Personal
Defense
for Women

Gila Hayes

Foreword by Massad Ayoob

613.66
Han

Published by

krause publications

A subsidiary of F+W Media, Inc.

700 East State Street • Iola, WI 54990-0001
715-445-2214 • 888-457-2873
www.krausebooks.com

Our toll-free number to place an order or obtain
a free catalog is (800) 258-0929.

Library of Congress Control Number: 2009923233

ISBN-13: 978-1-4402-0390-9
ISBN-10: 1-4402-0390-3

Designed by Kara Grundman
Edited by Dan Shideler

Printed in United States of America

OTHER RELATED TITLES

**The Gun Digest® Book of
Concealed Carry**
by Massad Ayoob

**The Gun Digest®
Book of Guns for Personal Defense**
edited by Kevin Michalowski

**The Gun Digest®
Book of Combat Handgunnery**
by Massad Ayoob

Effective Handgun Defense
by Frank W. James

FOREWORD

by Massad Ayoob

I t's an honor to write the foreword for Gila Hayes' latest book. She has long since emerged as one of the most articulate and influential voices in the movement toward effective self-protection for women.

Gila breaks the stereotypes. Those who oppose gun owners' civil rights in general and women's rights to protect themselves and their loved ones in particular, try to paint armed women as a cross between Tugboat Annie and a wanna-be Xena, The Warrior Princess. But when you meet Gila Hayes, you find a witty, self-possessed woman in prime of life who can debate articulately the choices she and so many other enlightened women have made…living proof that graceful femininity and strength are in no way mutually exclusive.

As a police weapons trainer since 1972, active in the national associations and attending international seminars, I've seen the best that great cadre has to offer. I can tell you that Gila is in the top tier of either gender, though she has become most famous for her ability to both inspire women to protect themselves and theirs, and effectively teach them how to do so. Cross-trained in less-lethal weapons, hand-to-hand, and the legal side, she puts the Armed Woman Lifestyle into a total, real-world perspective.

There's another stereotype that Gila absolutely shatters, the one that says, "Those who can, do, and those who can't, teach." Believe me, sisters and brothers, I've seen this woman shoot. I've seen her win women's shooting championships up to the national level, but perhaps more to the point, I've seen her win open championship titles, shooting against the men and beating them, with masculine stereotype weapons ranging from the .45 automatic to the 12 gauge shotgun. When she won the shotgun match one year at Washington State Law Enforcement Firearms Instructors' Seminar – shooting a hard-kicking Remington 870 pump with full-power slugs against big SWAT guys, some of whom were shooting reduced recoil loads in already soft-kicking semiautomatic shotguns – I wanted to dance in the streets. (I'm a father of daughters. Sue me. Our daughters need more role models like Gila Hayes.)

Read this book. Buy it for the ladies in your life, and urge them to read it too. It's not about guns so much as it's about empowerment.

ACKNOWLEDGMENTS

The ideas, principles and concepts making up this book are certainly not original with me. Training for armed self defense is a field that has been maturing since 1976 when Jeff Cooper, now deceased, opened Gunsite training academy to private citizens. I came to this study somewhat later, but did make it to Gunsite when the Colonel still came out on his ATV to see how classes were going. Though Cooper was no longer teaching then, his influence shines through the instruction of many of the leaders in firearms and tactical training today. I've been privileged to study with many of them: John Farnam, Clint Smith, Chuck Taylor, Ken Hackathorn, Louis Awerbuck and others.

In addition to Col. Cooper, another educator leaving an indelible stamp on the armed self defense movement is Massad Ayoob. He has quantified both the methods best suited to self defense shooting as well as the aftermath of a defense shooting. I have had the superb fortune to attend his classes for many years as a student, and as his assistant when he teaches at our school, The Firearms Academy of Seattle, Inc.

My guiding light and inspiration in those early years and through today is my husband Marty Hayes. It is to him that I dedicate the following pages. An innovative thinker, Marty's lifework in the field of firearms and tactical training and use of force doctrine is an interesting mix of innovation and conservatism. Without his urging and support, I would not have enjoyed the nearly two decades of writing magazine articles and two editions of my book *Effective Defense*.

The invitation to update and expand upon the materials I'd earlier published in *Effective Defense* came from Krause Publications editor

Dan Shideler at a most unexpected time. In early 2008, I had taken a sabbatical from magazine writing, in order to make time to get the new Armed Citizens' Legal Defense Network up and running. Even so, when Shideler called to ask if I'd like to do a women's armed defense book, I just couldn't resist. Trust me: without Shideler, the book you hold in your hands would not have been published. Thank you, Dan!

So many people pitched in to help illustrate this book that listing any one name opens up the danger that some will not be listed. The photographic illustrations are the work of the men behind the cameras: Grant Cunningham and Bob Jackson, without whom we would be facing dull pages of unrelieved type; Jacqueline Smith and Kathy Jackson (and several of her sons) willingly played a number of roles in varied scenarios; and folks helping out with other photos include the mom and daughter duo of Katie and Laurisa; Chris Cunningham; the Rahbani brothers; consummate "bad guy" Don Stahlnecker; Heath, McKenzie and Brady Gunns; Brenden Shellito, who generously opened his home to our photo crew; Tom and Diane Walls; Amy and Tycho Vosburgh; Jim Jacobe; and a goodly number of friends and students at the Firearms Academy of Seattle, Inc. who agreed to be photographed while they were training with us.

Any photos in which guns are pointed at role players use dummy guns, aluminum or plastic castings that have the general shape of a gun, or SIG Sauer's excellent Airsoft pistols, of which we make extensive use. We also use the tripod and remote controls for the camera in a number of live fire illustrations, to give the reader a different view of technique or equipment than is normally available.

But enough about the process. Let's get into the topic – how women can live safer lives! Thank you for your interest in this topic. It is my hope that the information in these pages can help you provide for your safety and that of your family.

Gila Hayes

January 28, 2009

CHAPTER *1*

Women's Rights and Responsibilities

I grew up with my mother's repertoire of fears: attack by strangers, kidnapping, rape, and other violence by men against women. She warned my sister and me to avoid strangers, to keep window shades down and never go out alone at night.

Yet never was there any mention of fighting back. We were taught to behave quietly, dress modestly and pray that you do not attract criminal attention. Our training was in avoidance; we had no game plan if evasion failed. Girls weren't taught how to fight, even in last-ditch self defense. We feared violence but weren't allowed to respond in kind.

Women now realize that rape and assault can happen to anyone, anywhere. Many women have wondered what they could do if attacked, and, finding no satisfactory answers, have tried to ignore the worry. It is unrealistic to hope that some good fortune will separate us from the estimated 50% of American women who are physically assaulted sometime in their lifetimes.[1]

Who's responsible?

In a world where women are responsible for earning their own living and often are sole support of their children, it is ironic that we have not fully embraced complete responsibility for our own self defense. Self-defense instructors report that the women most reluctant to acknowledge dangers and learn defensive tactics (whether a martial art or the handgun) are those who feel secure in their marriage or relationship. Newly single women, they tell me, are among their most enthusiastic students. It makes perfect sense: the newly independent person learns to enjoy many fresh challenges. Providing for her own survival offers much in strength, positive self-image and pride.

Relying on Uncle Sam

Gun control proponents want Americans to relinquish their weapons and rely on the government for protection, and unfortunately some of the loudest voices in the antigun campaign are female. Realistically, however, police forces are employed to patrol, maintain peace, and investigate crimes after the fact. Rarely do circumstances allow officers to stop a crime in progress.

This truth was emphasized way back in 1975, when three Washington, D.C women were raped, sodomized, and terrorized for fourteen hours in their home. A call went out to police in the initial moments of the attack. When four cruisers arrived at the home, the assailant prevented the women from answering the door and after five minutes the officers left. A second call received a promise of help on the way. Later investigation determined that officers were never dispatched to answer the second plea for help.

Fortunately, the women survived. Lawsuits ensued, and in 1981 the Court of Appeals for Washington, D.C., ruling on *Warren v. District of Columbia*, wrote that under American law the *"government and its agents are under no general duty to provide public services, such as police protection, to any individual citizen."*[2]

Too many women have been killed or injured while learning the bitter lesson that their restraining order is merely legal protection, not bodily defense. In 1989, a Los Angeles woman called 911 when threatened by her estranged husband, against whom she had a restraining order. When the dispatcher asked sarcastically if she expected a patrol car to park outside her home, Maria Navarro hung up. Within 30 minutes, a second call to 911 reported the murder of Navarro and a guest who was in her home to celebrate Navarro's birthday. Before police officers could arrive, her estranged husband killed another guest.

With a government that controls so many aspects of our lives, it is easy to understand how some come to believe themselves entitled to constant protection. Such expectations ignore estimates that the ratio of police officers to citizens is about 2.4 per 1000.[3] Realistically, no police department can respond instantly to every citizen's need, no matter how great an effort the officers make.

Learning to Be a Mother Wolf

When we rely on police and others to defend us, we perpetuate a society that perceives, trains, and treats women as unequal and as victims. When women are stereotyped as meek, defenseless prey, all women – from the bravest to the most timid – are are targets of victimization by strangers, acquaintances or mates.

To be female is to give life to the next generation. Instead of blindly accepting the traditional role of the weaker female, we must expand the feminine role to include defending life, as well as giving it birth. That means, after deliberation and training, that each woman should learn defenses against anyone who would injure her or take her life or harm those in her care, even if that defense entails taking or threatening the attacker's life.

The key is personal determination. Even the best self-defense weapon would be worthless without a woman's individual determination to preserve her own life and well-being at the expense of her assailant's life, if necessary.

If more women were willing to spill the blood of an assailant before sacrificing their own lives, I believe we would encounter fewer men

who are willing to risk injury or death for the gratification they achieve by abuse, rape and murder. In a survey published in 1986, over a third of felons questioned said they worried about being shot by their intended prey, and more than half agreed that "most criminals are more worried about meeting an armed victim than they are about running into the police."[4]

In my ideal world, anyone who assaults, terrorizes, or exploits a woman would run up against an individual of equal or superior defensive ability. How can this dream come true, when the female gender is physically smaller than the male? Disparity of force is ultimately balanced by mindset – the determination to defend one's life – and by training and acquiring the appropriate tools to support that determination.

Be a human version of mother wolf, willing to do whatever it takes to avoid harm to self or family. Here, responding to an unexpected knock at the door, Amy is ready for whatever is there.

The bottom line? We are individually responsible for our own survival and well-being. Just as a healthy woman exercises and eats wholesome food, a woman needs to prepare herself for the eventuality that she may need to defend herself and her loved ones against assault. Until we embrace our responsibility to survive, we continue to fuel the violence and abuse that threaten our peace and safety.

Notes

[1] Full Report of the Prevalence, Incidence and Consequences of Violence Against Women, citing finding of the National Violence Against Women Survey, reported by the Department of Justice in November 2000.

[2] *Warren v. Dist. of Columbia, D.C.* App., 444 A.2d 1 (1981).

[3] Federal Bureau of Investigation Crime Report, www.fbi.gov/ucr/cius2006/

[4] Wright, J. & Rossi, P., *Armed and Considered Dangerous: A Survey of Felons and their Firearms* (1986), published by Aldine de Guyter Press; based on data from a survey formerly released by the National Institute of Justice.

Developing a Safety-Conscious Attitude

Animals wisely put their physical survival before other considerations. Far more in touch with survival instincts than are we, the so-called "lesser creatures" often avoid danger with greater skill. Humans are tempted to deny the existence of danger or, if we do admit it, we usually follow it up with "I know, but –"

" – but I can't afford a reliable car."

" – but I can't afford an apartment in a safe, secure building."

" – but I can't pay for self defense training and a weapon."

Others who acknowledge the risk stop training short of the level of skill required to deal with a determined assailant. Early in my karaté training, I hoped I could fight off a one-on-one assault, although I was worried that two or more assailants could overpower me. I had to be thrown to the mat a number of times before acknowledging that at that skill level, I could easily be overcome by just one. I needed more skills and additional weapon choices.

After a woman acknowledges the danger, she needs to obtain the skills and weapons that will allow her to go where she needs while still behaving with reasonable safety. What choices will she make that give her the maximum safety with the least restrictions? A hermit-like withdrawal from the daily threats of modern living is rarely practical or satisfactory. Instead, I am advising a critical, realistic assessment of your world and pragmatic decisions based on its dangers.

Judith Weiss, a self-defense instructor I met through our mutual membership in the American Women's Self-Defense Association (now the Association for Women's Self-Defense Advancement[1]), offers the following explanation:

"All activities (driving a car, filling the bathtub, walking through the parking lot at night) entail some risk. We all have different attitudes toward risk. At one end of the scale is refusing to engage in an activity by exaggerating the risk involved. At the other end is engaging in very risky activities while refusing to take any precautions. Neither of these attitudes is useful for living an empowered life. What is useful is to accurately assess the risks involved, take whatever precautions make sense, and live as fully as possible."

Women of all ages, even these high schoolers, choose the image they present to the world. One cries out for attention from one and all, the other suggests self-confidence and control.

Ask yourself now: what compromises am I willing to make to assure my well-being? While living outside the United States for a time, I learned to blend in to avoid the hassles faced by a woman traveling alone. That habit, plus growing older and a declining sensitivity about others' opinions, has eased me into a comfortable style of dress that doesn't scream out for attention. Understand this well: if you want to be noticed, be assured you will receive attention from one and all, not just from sane, desirable people.

My own beautiful sister told me of the day she realized this truth. "I was unloading the trunk of my car," she explained. In the heat of summer, she wore short cutoffs that attracted the attention of a vagrant. "Hey, sister, you sure do keep yourself in good shape," she heard in a slurred male voice. Acknowledging him with a surprised, "Thank you," she rushed to the safety of her nearby destination.

I well understand that this advice sounds like the common accusation that a woman "asks to be assaulted" by how she dresses. This, of course, is absurd. Predators select victims for a variety of reasons. But you must also choose how you will deal with unwanted comments and even being followed by odd strangers as a side-effect of your choice of appearance. If you make this choice, do it consciously, understanding the results and possible dangers. If you will make different choices, I recommend reserving your Spandex for the gym, keeping your short shorts at home, and covering your sports bra with a T-shirt when in public. Showy or expensive jewelry can also attract trouble.

Only the Strong Survive?

Predatory people can intuitively sniff out those they can overpower psychologically or physically. They observe body posture and levels of alertness. This was underscored by a New York study in which prisoners convicted of assault watched a videotape of random strangers on the street, then rated how likely they would be to assault them. When the prisoners described a victim profile for women they might assault, they cited 1) slouching posture, 2) head held down, 3) eyes averted, and 4) a shuffling pace instead of brisk walk.[2]

Though few advance far enough in their training to mount a decisive unarmed defense against a committed assailant, the martial arts can transform bodies and attitudes. Karaté was the catalyst that changed my timid, submissive posture into an erect, confident stance that I know discourages assailants and predators.

A common characteristic shared by most vulnerable women is unawareness of threats. A careless woman will wander right into the arms of trouble, engrossed in conversation or simply lost in her own thoughts and worries. Unfortunately, nearly all the people I know suffer from a lack of awareness of their moment-to-moment surroundings. If you can't answer a pop-quiz about the area you passed through five minutes ago, you are caught in this oblivion. Inner contemplation is good, but not on the street where being deep in thought can cost your life. The woman who indulges in air-headedness experiences an immobilizing terror when surprised by danger.

States of Awareness: White, Yellow, Orange, Red and Black Conditions

I call it absolute awareness: the acknowledgment that danger exists, coupled with moment-to-moment watchfulness. Many schools of armed self defense employ the late Colonel Jeff Cooper's color code to describe the states of awareness appropriate to different levels of threat. Col. Cooper, known to handgunners as the father of modern pistolcraft, adapted the color code used in military operations during World War II, when radio-transmitted reports on troop conditions were subject to interception by the enemy. Instructors, including Massad Ayoob, have altered the code slightly to better suit the private citizen's choices of preclusion or retreat.

CONDITION WHITE describes circumstances in which you are completely oblivious to any threat. One enters Condition White in sleep or when daydreaming as discussed earlier.

This woman is quite oblivious to a trap that is being set for her. She is in Condition White.

Though not alerted to a specific danger yet, this woman's awareness causes her to assess others occupying the area next to her parking area. She is in Condition Yellow.

A heightened level of awareness to the potential danger from someone coming into her personal space takes this woman to Condition Orange.

As the assailant reveals his knife, his intended victim shifts into Condition Red, creating distance and seeking an obstacle to serve as cover.

Defender, in Condition Black, takes appropriate action to the assault that is underway.

Awareness to the *potential* for danger, even without any recognizable threat, is CONDITION YELLOW. Psychologists tell us that humans can spend all their waking hours in Condition Yellow with absolutely no detrimental effects. Indeed, Condition Yellow should be your mental state while driving, chopping up vegetables, or hammering a nail into the wall. You are not threatened by any immediate danger, but you're aware that your activity includes potential hazards that you watchfully avoid.

Some activities are riskier than others. Circumstances may prompt you to switch into CONDITION ORANGE. This attitude is appropriate in situations that entail a higher degree of risk, such as driving on icy roads or entering your empty home late at night. In Condition Orange, all your senses are active, scanning for potential danger. You are prepared to take appropriate action should a specific threat appear.

If, for example, an armed stranger approaches as you unlock your front door, you switch to CONDITION RED, in which you have identified a specific life-threatening danger.

If Condition Red is embodied in the thought, "Oh, no, he *could* assault me!" CONDITION BLACK is "He *is* assaulting me now!" Condition Black indicates that a lethal assault is in progress and justifies immediate use of any level of force necessary to stop the assault.

How does the defensive firearm fit into these conditions? In Condition White you should not have a lethal weapon such as a gun available, since your lack of alertness makes the weapon vulnerable to an assailant or to a child's misuse. Secure it in a lock box or gun safe, since in Condition White you are not in command of its power. In Condition Yellow you may or may not have your weapon readily available; however if you do have one, you must not drift into the unguarded Condition White. In Condition Orange it would be preferable to have immediate access to your weapon or alternative defenses, like a trained guard dog at your side. Depending on the situation, the weapon may or may not be in your hand. In Condition

Red the weapon should be in your hand if circumstances permit. You need to be ready and able to use it if a lethal assault pushes you into Condition Black.

Guns Won't Keep You Safe

What? A firearms instructor saying that a gun won't keep you safe? Yes, ma'am! *Absolute awareness about your surroundings, tactical planning, and ability with an appropriate weapon are the factors that will keep you alive and well.* You are the active party – your gun is an inert mechanical assembly, incapable of any action on its own.

A gun or any other defensive device is useless if the owner is oblivious to threat. The prepared woman, however, besides maintaining an appropriate level of awareness, will study, practice and perfect her defense tactics.

Notes

[1]Association for Women's Self-Defense Advancement, 556 Ft. 17 N., Ste. 7-209, Paramus, NJ 07652 http://awsda.org 1-800-STOP RAPE

[2]Betty Grayson and Morris I. Stein, "Attracting Assault: Victims Non Verbal Cues; *Journal of Communication*, March 1981.

CHAPTER 3

A Fight Avoided Is a Fight Won

O ver-socialized humans are rarely prepared to respond instantly to assault. It is a tremendous shock to find a punch coming toward your face or find yourself immobilized by a bear-hug from behind. This element of surprise serves criminal assailants well, whether they attack men or women. Mental preparation coupled with physical training gives the advantage or edge that avoids, escapes or wins the fight. There are few places it is safe to lapse into Condition White.

Know who and what are around you. Practice this exercise: when driving or walking, train yourself to see all the details, all the people, doorways, windows and natural elements like thick foliage. Mentally re-create the scene through which you just passed as though designing a movie set. In your mind, describe the people inside a distance of 20 feet; describe cars and structures; detail objects you could use as bullet-stopping cover in a gunfight or obstacles to prevent physical contact with an assailant. As awareness of the scene ahead and around you becomes habitual, you'll rarely be startled by the wino that lurches out of the doorway to ask for money. You will already have moved to the outside of the sidewalk, insulated among other pedestrians.

Jacqueline's alert demeanor brought this hazard to her attention in time to step to the far side of the alley providing distance from an uncertain situation.

Asking for assistance is a common ploy the criminal uses to gain control over the victim. When strangers approach, it is impossible to predict their motives.

The Defensive Posture

Walk purposefully, head up, eyes scanning your surroundings. Keep your hands free so you are ready to fight if surprised. Don't shove your hands into pockets or wrap your arms around your torso. Whenever possible, avoid carrying a big purse or filling your arms with packages. Briefcases, laptop computer bags and luggage need shoulder straps. Keep your limbs supple and relaxed, ready to move quickly. Stay loose and alert.

Advice about eye contact varies. I suggest making brief eye contact with other pedestrians. A student once told me that the state social agency for which she worked advised employees to avoid eye contact, suggesting that it inflames mentally unstable subjects. I replied that it is important to communicate by brief eye contact that you are aware of another's presence. This differs from a hard stare that communicates aggression. Let potential predators know you have recognized them for what they are. Abusers prefer anonymity. Walk away from comments from strangers and let compliments, criticism and other unsolicited communication pass unanswered.

Learn a few basic rules for dealing with aggressive approaches from strangers. Whether overseas or in America, one of the most common approaches a criminal takes is to ask an innocent question. The problem is, it never ends with the first question. The predator prolongs the exchange, asking other questions about landmarks or events, anything to distract you until they have a chance to slip through your defenses and get what they want: your possessions or your person. A stranger will approach you in a parking lot, asking, "Excuse me, do you know the way to the bus station?" Without pausing, make eye contact and firmly shake your head "no." Most toward the nearest safe place and let the person know you will not tolerate further encroachment into your safety zone.

Experience tells me that ignoring a harasser is usually perceived as fearfulness. Make eye contact, politely and forcefully answer that you cannot help them. Maintain a safe distance. Assaults happen lightning fast – usually in three to five seconds. Too often the female prey is knocked to the ground before she realizes what is happening.

Where Is It Written That You Have to Be Friendly to Strangers?

While the Bible directs believers to turn the other cheek and to love thy neighbor as thyself, nowhere does it advocate sacrificing innocent life for the gratification of evildoers. Today's reality requires a guarded response to strangers. Giving help to those in need is admirable, but it can and must be accomplished in sensible, safe ways.

Two of our century's most notorious mass killers, Alton Coleman and his accomplice Debra Denise Brown, approached a number of victims by asking for rides to church or prayer meetings. The victims were robbed, raped and usually murdered by the criminal pair. Serial rapist-murderer Theodore Bundy viciously exploited the human desire to help others by pretending to be injured. It is thought that he accomplished his first double-murder by asking women at a lake near Seattle to help him load a boat onto his car. They believed he needed help with the task because he wore an arm sling. After capturing one young woman with this ruse, Bundy returned and successfully abducted a second victim.

How to avoid falling victim to this sort of ploy? First, recognize the predatory stalking technique of stepping in close and engaging the prey in unnecessary conversation. If circumstances don't allow an immediate escape from your stalker, face your harasser and order in a firm, loud voice: "Go away! Don't talk to me!" or "Leave me alone, now!" Couple your command with forceful eye contact. Communicate through your unwavering gaze, showing your assailant you are not afraid to take whatever action is necessary to rid yourself of him. Use a decisive, commanding voice.

The first women's self-defense course I ever took, many years ago, taught us to cuss and swear loudly at assailants. The premise was

When no alternative to the parking garage exists, choose the safest parking spot near an exit and walk well away from cars that may conceal a predator. This woman keeps her coat open so she can get to her holstered handgun easily if it is needed.

that the foul language would shock the harasser into breaking off the pursuit. Experience has since shown that gutter language has little effect, it may escalate the assault, and it will certainly make you appear to be the instigator or an active participant in the fight. Witnesses will perceive abusive language as active involvement in a two-sided dispute.

If your assailant disregards your command to leave, take evasive action if you have not already tried to escape. In crowded public spaces, uninvolved bystanders can serve as a distraction while you get away. Move around other pedestrians so they and others have to step between you and your harasser, giving you time to escape. Other urban features that provide escape routes are people-filled malls, stores and public buildings. Here, buffered by onlookers, you may be able to disappear into the crowd.

There are no winners in a street fight. At close quarters and against a committed fighter, even taking a gun to a knife fight may not save you. The knifer may die from your bullet, yet not before he has cut you repeatedly with his blade. *Always try to escape a confrontation; join the fight only if the alternative is unavoidable death or crippling injury.*

React decisively if your instincts tell you something is wrong. If you feel scared or uneasy, leave the area. Be prepared to fight back immediately and viciously if you are assaulted. A small revolver in your pocket, a can of pepper spray or a mini-baton or keys in your hand may deflect an assailant long enough for you to reach safety or deploy another weapon. Whatever your defensive tools, their value is only as great as your pre-established defensive plan. Have simple, vicious responses planned and mentally rehearsed: "I will do 'A' if that person does 'B'."

Danger Signs

Ability to react dynamically relies on recognizing danger before it is on top of you. Too often denial or air-headedness blinds women to predictable predatory approaches. As outlined earlier, Condition

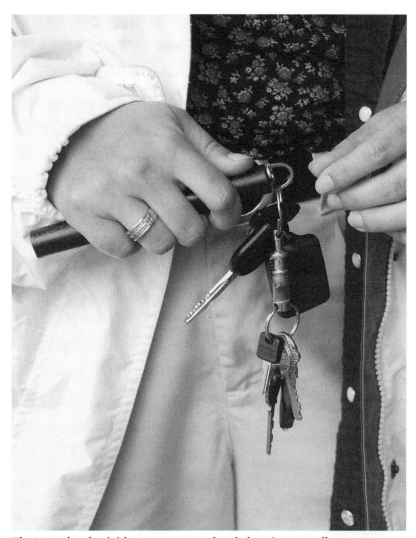

The Monadnock mini-baton serves as a handy key ring, as well as a very serviceable intermediate defensive tool that can be carried openly without attracting attention.

Yellow codifies the appropriate level of awareness vital to knowing what threats may be present. Your guard should go up if an attempt is made to block your path – whether as a pedestrian or driver. By maintaining a good danger scan, this ploy is avoidable. Observed far enough ahead, you have room to cross the street rather than step into an alley or bushes to get around an impediment.

It is essential that you know what people around you are doing. Take care that you are not "blinded" by your stereotype of what a "typical" criminal looks like. Be aware of teens and young adults of either gender, as well as people in all manner of dress and grooming. Be alert to followers who match your pace, pausing when you do or walking faster to keep up with you.

A car that follows you slowly or pulls ahead and stops near the sidewalk should raise an alert. A car that has passed you several times is cause for concern. Unless an escape route is accessible, do not look away if you're targeted: the predators have already chosen you. Instead, pointedly look inside the car, do your best to memorize features or characteristics of those inside and get the license plate number. Remember, anonymity, not recognition, serves the criminal.

Be aware of predatory teamwork in which one member distracts you as the other attacks. Look for exchanged glances, nods or signals between two pedestrians who do not appear to be together; watch out for circling or flanking moves. A stranger who pushes or bumps you should generate a high level of watchfulness on your part, and not just toward the offender. The contact may be a distractionary move to channel you into a partner's grasp, or it may indicate mental instability, intoxication, or simply a rude, aggressive person with whom exchanging words may lead to an unexpected confrontation. Whatever the problem, you do not have to become part of it.

Likewise, move away from drunken or boisterous groups to avoid being the prey of dog-pack mentality. In many situations, a wise tactic is to interpose obstacles between yourself and the threat. This may be as simple as stepping around others in a crowd, crossing a busy street, or stepping around a parked car to place it between yourself and the danger. A large planter, trash container or any other object may prevent the person you fear from rushing you. Absence of crowds is poor reason to let down your guard. All an empty street assures is the absence of witnesses.

Faced by any of these predictable predatory warning cues, wishing that it "ain't so" won't change anything. Do something, and do it NOW to avoid, escape, or – if necessary – strike back before you are injured.

Choose Your Pleasures

A woman must weigh the events she attends to determine if they entail a greater-than-ordinary threat because of location or the type of crowd. Is the level of threat manageable under the circumstances surrounding the event? For example, I might skip a popular concert, since concert security personnel usually frisk spectators, making it impossible to carry a defense weapon. I might decline to attend an evening theatre production held in a neighborhood with a high crime rate. These decisions are extensions of the acknowledgment that dangers exist. They represent the mindset embodied in Condition Yellow, in which you consciously avoid that which might cause you harm.

Choose your dangers. For example, I despise huge multi-floor concrete parking garages. I'm not the only one who feels at risk going there. A clerk at a gun range told me that after feeling threatened in a hospital's underground parking facility, he started parking on the street or in an open-air lot, even though it was considerably less convenient. A 2005 Department of Justice study of violent crimes found that a bit over 8% of crimes of violence happened in parking lots or garages.[1] Many parking garages don't generate enough foot traffic to provide the relative safety of crowds and aren't patrolled nearly often enough to deter the opportunist looking for a victim.

If you must park in public garages, walk in the driving lane, avoiding the close confines and concealment between parked cars, and have your gun immediately accessible. Park in a garage with live attendants and drive right back out if anything looks or feels threatening once you are inside. Park near the attendant and in a brightly lit area. If you are delayed at work until the garage is empty, ask a trusted coworker or a security officer who you know to escort you to your car. Follow your instincts: they will keep you alive.

Public elevators are another location in which I exercise guarded caution. A few years ago, I'm told, numerous Seattle women began using the stairs after a series of muggings and molestations in the downtown high-rise elevators. These women exercised admirable awareness of danger, and probably got a little extra muscle tone as a bonus. Seriously, give me a crowded elevator, with all its discomforts, instead of an elevator car containing only one or two people. Don't board an elevator with a single occupant; wait for the next car. When you get in an elevator, stand near the control panel, keeping a weapon in hand: a revolver in the pocket, or your Persuader mini-baton or your keys held ready in your hand.

I see women taking more risks while jogging and exercising than during nearly any other activity. Women exercise along deserted running paths, in parks replete with hiding spots, and wearing garments that a courtroom lawyer can construe as sexually inviting. Again, I don't advocate locking yourself away in a cloister: I do suggest responsible awareness. If possible, walk or jog with several companions and a protective dog. Even in groups, maintain awareness of your surroundings, don't drift off in a haze of burning muscles or music from your MP3 player. I would not cut off my auditory warning system by wearing headphones in public, whether jogging, riding the bus or waiting in a queue.

Jogging paths are a more difficult subject. Many running paths follow scenic, yet remote and dangerous, routes. Bushes, trees and ravines offer concealment for an assailant and a place to which he may drag his victims. In urban areas, jog on a public track around an open playing field. And use the track only during daylight and at times when other people are about.

Automobile Safety AAA Never Told You About

The aware woman uses everyday equipment to maintain her safety, understanding that a weapon is actually a very small part of the personal safety equation. A locked car surrounds you with an added ring of safety, if you are alert to tactical advantages. Maintaining a safe car that will not fail you is critical. This, as with home safety, is a matter of priorities. Forego buying a new pair of shoes in favor of getting a tune up. Keep the gas tank more than a quarter full, so you don't absent-mindedly run out of gas and become stranded. Exercise alertness at gas stations, observing the area carefully before starting to pump gas and remaining aware of the surroundings while pumping. Chose a pump at which you cannot be blocked in from front and rear, and use a credit card to pay at the pump as a way to minimize your exposure and time out of your car's safety.

Actually, your safety begins before you get in the car. Your personal vehicle should always remain locked, even when you are in it. Look beneath the car from a distance while approaching, and check between the seats for an intruder before getting inside. Once in the car, lock all the doors to keep unwanted "passengers" out. Never pick up hitchikers or allow a stranger into your car. If flagged down to help at an apparent emergency, remain in your locked car and call the highway patrol for assistance. Drive away after reporting the location and situation.

Learn basic car maintenance skills such as changing tires. The ability to replace a flat tire and get your car to a service station greatly increases your safety. (Keeping a can of Fix-A-Flat tire inflator handy can literally be a lifesaver.) *If you cannot repair the car's problem, do not leave the safety of your locked car.* If you have a cell phone, dial 911 to summon help. If not, put up the hood and wait inside your locked car for the state patrol. Do not open the door or window for anyone but an identified law enforcement officer. If, for any reason, you are unsure of the officer's legitimacy, remain in the car and ask him to call a tow truck.

When you are stopped at a traffic light, glance around to see who and what is within striking distance. At traffic lights, maintain distance between your car and the one ahead. A good visual cue is to stay far enough back to see the rear tires of the car ahead. This space will allow you to pull around the car and escape if an attack is initiated while you are stopped. If first in line at the light on a multilane street, leave half a car length between you and the stop line. Most drivers will simply stop somewhat ahead of you, increasing your anonymity and making you a less attractive target to the occupants of cars in the adjacent lanes. And, by the way, before pulling out into that intersection when the light changes, check in both directions then count "thousand one, thousand two," to be sure the yellow-to-red light jumpers all get through before you drive through, as wisely advocated by Curt Rich in his outstanding book *Drive to Survive!*[2] which I highly recommend.

While driving, remain alert to cars that may be following you. Taking down a license plate number and checking in the rear view mirror may discourage an opportunistic assailant who prefers easier prey. If you are followed, do not go home. Make at least three right- or left-hand turns, then go to the nearest occupied public facility, stop, close to the door and run inside, calling out loudly, "Call the police, I'm being stalked!"

If you are attacked while stopped in traffic, take any escape route

Don't get blocked in. Leave enough room between your bumper and theirs that you can pull around the car in front of you, even if blocked from behind.

If space allows, you may be able to speed away from a carjacking attempt with greater chances of survival than if you get out and take your chances with the gunman.

available – at times like this it's OK to break traffic laws. While you must remain aware of others' safety, you need not sit immobile at a red light and allow a window to be broken in by an assailant, instead of driving through an empty intersection or onto the sidewalk.

In fact, simply speeding away from a carjacking attempt is one of the methods I've seen demonstrated by executive protection professionals in training and practice. If the car drives away rapidly enough, it's nearly impossible for the bad guy to keep a good sight picture on the car's occupants. While the assailant could spray the area with gunfire, that attracts attention and you are safer than if you got out of the car and got into a fight with the attacker. While there's nothing wrong with the advice to give up the car if it makes sense, there may be times when a car-seated child or other complication makes driving away rapidly the better strategy.

Gun against gun, not good survival odds. It would be better to get that car moving!

On longer stretches of freeway or rural highway, a car that matches your speed and hangs alongside yours should at least raise your level of concern. It may be a road-weary motorist or it may be a predator. If another driver's actions alarm you, exit at the next ramp and drive to a busy gas station or other public facility. If followed, you have a much better idea of what you are up against. Before stopping, make at least three turns to determine if you are truly being followed, then call for help. A cell phone is mandatory equipment in a car. Use it to call 911, giving a full description of your harasser, location and your circumstances. Be sure of your location by noting street names and landmarks while making the several turns to verify you are indeed being followed,

We have all been taught, from Driver's Ed onward, to get out of the car if involved in a minor accident. Predators recognize this tendency as an opportunity. The rapist causes a fender bender and attacks when you leave the safety of your car to inspect the damage. Remaining in your car is much safer, and you may wait for the police to arrive, or drive to a busy, well-lit area to report the accident from a safe place. Under no conditions should you get out of your car if only you and the other driver are on the scene. I would hesitate to get out of my car if a second motorist stopped to assist, recognizing the risk of criminal teamwork. I would ask the "Good Samaritan" to go call for help, remaining safely inside the car until the police arrived.

Never stop to help what appears to be a stranded motorist, even if it looks like a lone woman. You simply cannot know their disposition, true identity or if there are accomplices hidden where you cannot see them. If you feel you should help, call the police, who will respond and help those who are truly stranded.

Taking the Bus

If you use bus transportation, try to establish a schedule that lets you use the bus during daylight. If that's not possible, board and disembark at stops that are busy and well lit. On the bus, be alert

– know who is on the bus, what they're doing and how close they are to you. Try to sit in the front near the driver, and make an effort to break through the anonymity of being "just one of the passengers," if the driver seems trustworthy. On the bus, be very wary of strangers who strike up uninvited conversation or try to elicit information about your destination, or where you live or work. Also be aware that your personal conversations may be overheard and exploited.

When disembarking from public transportation, watch to see who exits with you. If evasive action, such as crossing a street several times, does not discourage your follower, run to the nearest populated and well-lit area yelling, "Help! Call the police! I'm being followed. Call the police!"

Choose Safety

In every situation, the aware woman will ask herself, "Does it feel safe?" She will mentally explore the potential for danger before committing herself to any action. For example, if asked to visit the home of a new male friend, the aware woman will probably respond that she is sorry, she cannot, but she may counter with an invitation to get together in a restaurant or other public location. A responsible man will recognize her prudence without taking offense; a predator will vocally express insult, take offense or ridicule her caution. Consider this episode a good test to find out if your new friend will respect your intelligence and sensibility.

Sometimes, however, despite our best intentions, we have no alternative to the use of deadly force. With that sobering fact in mind, let's move on to specific survival considerations.

Notes

[1] U.S. Department of Justice, Bureau of Justice Statistics: http://www.ojp.usdoj.gov/bjs/abstract/cvusst.htm

[2] Rich, Curt, *Drive to Survive!,* ISBN 0-7603-0525-0, 1998, MBI Publishing Co., 729 Prospect Ave., P. O. Box 1, Osceola, WI 54020.

CHAPTER 4

Finding the Will to Survive

C ould you harm someone else in order to preserve your own life?

In my own case, that question finally left my mind after an immersion study of justifiable use of deadly force. I recommend similar studies for women plagued with questions about of their ability to use deadly force in self defense. At a minimum, obtain Tanya Metaksa's book *Safe, Not Sorry*[1] and read it well. Read and reread Massad Ayoob's *In the Gravest Extreme* and attend his seminars if possible.

Initially, my determination to fight back became stronger through firearms training that included videotaped lectures by Ayoob, an

authority on the lawful use of deadly force. His frank discussions of the danger, illustrated by case histories and their adjudication in American courts, confirmed my belief that I was at risk and at the same time strengthened my resolve to protect myself. The study forced me to confront a fear of attack that has

Massad Ayoob, a dynamic and animated speaker, lectures on judicious use of deadly force.

been with me since earliest childhood. In the end, I became convinced of my responsibility to stop any threat to my life and of my own right to survival.

I still find it hard to listen to story after story of victimization and assault, but my immersion in this study of self defense has burned away the emotional baggage of feeling powerless.

I'm not powerless. Neither are you.

Deciding to Live

The will to fight has been trained out of socialized humans. If surprised by an assailant, do not expect some defensive instinct to surface automatically. If you have not confronted issues about your right to defend yourself, questions of legality and morality may be foremost in your mind, interfering with the concentration that should be directing your defense. I don't think an ethical person can blithely say, "Sure, it's no problem to kill to save my own life" and fail to pursue an understanding what it means to kill in self defense.

Read the work of Ayoob and John Farnam.[2] Obtain Robert A. Waters' *The Best Defense: True Stories of Intended Victims Who Defended Themselves With a Firearm*[3] and read Chris Bird's *Thank God I Had A Gun*.[4] Study the experiences of those who have been forced to use guns in self defense and consider what they have experienced in the aftermath. Give serious thought to reports of citizens' self-defense acts as reported in the NRA's monthly "Armed Citizen" columns, and in *Combat Handguns, Concealed Carry Magazine* and other publications.

Fundamental to the self-defense mindset is this: The assail*ant forfeits his right to live by initiating an assault likely to kill or cripple an innocent person. The fault is the perpetrator's, not the victim's.*

A woman's determination to fight back grows stronger with an understanding of the conditions under which the law and society condone use of deadly force. Killing to protect property will reap a grave punishment both in the courts and in the reaction of family, friends, neighbors, employers and others. And though killing in self defense is also likely to earn societal disapproval, clear-cut cases of self defense are court-defensible. The survivor can deal with the resulting social fallout because she is alive to do so.

A serious study of use of deadly force yields a mature conviction to use this ultimate power only to preserve innocent life, not to threaten or intimidate. "The Decision," as this process is termed by Ayoob, is one that assigns the ultimate value to innocent human life, not to self-image, pride or material possessions.

Make no mistake: this is not a decision to become a cold-blooded killer; this is a resolution to preserve that unique spark of life that is you.

It's a typical Sunday afternoon as mom Laurisa plays with her daughter Katie. Dave the puppy's sharp teeth are cause for more immediate concern than the Glock 26 she carries for home defense, yet she is prepared to protect the family should real danger threaten.

The Mental Process

As you begin to clarify your own determination to survive, you may find yourself idly considering various scenarios concerning assault and self-defense. Defined by Ayoob as a process of inoculation, most experience it when beginning to grasp what constitutes righteous self defense. This seems to be the mind's way of resolving ideas that run counter to our earliest training to "do no harm" or "turn the other cheek." These thoughts and mental images are your social conscience weighing the propriety of your newly-embraced determination to survive. The best advice I can offer is to accept the process.

Don't judge yourself harshly for these thoughts. Understand that your mind is weighing the unfair constraints society has imposed on women for far too long against your new belief that you have the right to survive unmolested.

One of my students once told me that although she had no nightmares during her first months of carrying a gun, she was weighed down with guilt because she thoroughly enjoyed shooting. She said it seemed terrible to like something capable of deadly results. Like all of us, she needed the company of like-minded individuals who could share similar experiences and confirm that the pleasure of shooting practice was not an expression of an evil side.

Other students have reported uneasiness and feelings of unspecified anxiety, as they grapple with the concept of using deadly force in self defense, or even just possessing a deadly weapon. Women often report that friends and family are horrified by their interest in guns, contributing to their feelings of general disapproval.

Sometimes it's difficult finding another woman with whom you can discuss such things. Responsible armed citizens, particularly women, belong to an extremely limited peer group who will do what is necessary to prevent rape, murder or violent assault. Our feminine support group is miniscule! Beyond the practical aspect of training, shooting classes can provide fellowship with like-minded people. A class that meets your needs will likely contain other women who are dealing with many of the same issues. Women's self-defense groups listed below can put you in contact with groups and instructors who share your concerns.[5]

Our Innate Advantage

At last, it is time for the good news: women are far less likely than men to be damned by society and their peers if forced to use a gun to stop a rape or assault. Men are often burdened with the macho ideal that they must fight fairly, man-to-man. Society's stereotypical portrayal of the helpless female actually justifies her need to use deadly force against a rapist or murderer.

These women take an afternoon to try out one another's guns and enjoy the company of like-minded women.

Two female students listen intently as Massad Ayoob teaches his StressFire shooting method.

As a result, the woman who has determined to pull the trigger in self defense may act more decisively if faced with an assailant who intends her harm. After the assault, she will suffer less condemnation from society and will face fewer accusations that she used excessive force to save her life.

Notes

[1]Metaksa, Tanya, *Safe, Not Sorry*, 1997 HarperCollins Publishers, Inc., 10 East 53rd St., New York, NY 10022.

[2]Massad Ayoob's *In the Gravest Extreme* and *The Ayoob Files,* and John Farnam's *The Street Smart Gun Book* can be found in retail gun stores or by order from Police Bookshelf, 800-624-9049, www.ayoob.com.

[3]Waters, Robert A., *The Best Defense*, Cumberland House Publishing, 431 Harding Industrial Park Drive, Nashville, TN 37211, 888-439-2665.

[4]Bird, Chris, *Thank God I Had a Gun*, Privateer Publications, P. O. Box 29427, San Antonio, TX 78229 210-308-8191, www.privateer publications.com

[5]Arming Women Against Rape and Endangerment (AWARE), P.O. Box 242, Bedford, MA 01730-0242; Association for Women's Self-Defense Advancement, 556 Ft. 17 N., Ste. 7-209, Paramus, NJ 07652 http://awsda.org 1-888-STOP RAPE.; National Rifle Association of America, Women's Issues and Information, 11250 Waples Mill Road, Fairfax, VA 22030 703-267-1413; Second Amendment Sisters, 900 RR 620 South, Ste. C101, PMB 228, Lakeway, TX 78734, www.2aSisters. org; *Women & Guns Magazine*, P. O. Box 35, Buffalo, NY 14205, 716-885-6408, www.womenandguns.

CHAPTER 5

Emotional and Physical Consequences of Survival

A survivor who employs deadly force in self defense must prevail in several arenas: physical, legal and emotional. The news media dissects self-defense shootings and other tragedies with little regard for the survivor's feelings; in the courts, lawyers argue about the circumstances and second-guess the survivor's actions; and the survivor herself must come to terms with the assault and her act of self defense. You don't hear much about emotional recovery from a violent event, only physical recovery.

I intentionally emphasized the word "survivor" in the first sentence above. Society has difficulty equating "victim" with "survivor," yet the person who is forced to shoot or otherwise fight in self defense is simultaneously victim of a crime to which she did not contribute, and at the same time, its survivor.

The emotional aftermath largely results from our society's reaction to killing and is made worse by the physiological response to the monumental stress of a life-death emergency. The leader on post-violent event trauma is police psychologist Dr. Walter Gorski. Though he has published no books, his professional papers and studies have been distilled and taught extensively by leading instructors such as Massad Ayoob and John Farnam, and are the basis for this chapter. A "must-see" reference is Calibre Press' video *Ultimate Survivors*[1] which re-enacts the stories of several law enforcement professionals who survived deadly assaults and lived to relate their experiences and to discuss the aftermath.

The Aftermath

After a self-defense emergency, the survivor's body must eliminate the adrenaline produced during the crisis. Adrenaline is a powerful hormone requiring hours to leave the body, and its side effects are the some of the first post-violent event trauma symptoms the survivor experiences. Directly after an emergency, adrenaline creates agitation and a heightened mental state that may be followed by nausea or lethargy.

Survival puts a different perspective on day-to-day needs such as food and sleep. Sleeplessness may continue for several nights after a crisis. Nightmares commonly afflict those surviving a violent event. The dreams are often terrifying replays of the assault, with endless variations, bizarre twists and conclusions. During waking hours, daydreams or flashbacks also replay the event.

Assault survivors generally suffer insomnia, first as the adrenaline leaves the body, and later as the mind sorts through the horror of the attack. Likewise, loss or exaggeration of appetite may occur after a life-threatening emergency. Those who are treated by several professionals simultaneously may receive conflicting medications. If simultaneously receiving help from a psychiatrist and a physician, tell each professional about other treatment, and advise them of prescriptions you have been given to avoid receiving conflicting drugs. Alcohol or drug dependency is a pitfall. Mental health professional

Arthur Mize taught me that alcohol use suppresses the brain function critical to processing and coming to terms with the trauma, making post-traumatic stress disorder far more likely.

Many shooting survivors experience sexual dysfunction or promiscuity and relationships or marriages sometimes fall apart after a shooting. Besides sexual difficulties, the relationship may be challenged by the survivor's need for introspection, excluding the partner who desperately wants to assist in the loved one's recovery, for he, too, has nearly lost a precious part of his life. The survivor, however, often feels emotionally isolated, believing that no one understands her doubts and emotions.

The isolation increases if friends stop visiting the survivor. Just as you may have searched for the words to comfort one who has lost someone to death, others may struggle to interact with a friend who has killed in self defense. Despite their concern, acquaintances often clam up, fearful that they will say something to upset the survivor. Those who act as if nothing has happened risk the survivor's outrage at the suggestion that the shooting was a casual event. Others become impatient with the excess precaution and fear of one who has survived a violent assault.

Affection and patience are required. While friends and acquaintances need not be counselors, they can give priceless assurance and support to a survivor who is struggling to overcome an uninformed public's judgments about her decision to save her life.

Surviving a self-defense shooting is a long and arduous process. Healing can be facilitated by skilled counseling, so don't try to survive alone. A counselor, spiritual advisor or physician offers the survivor solace and assistance during the emotional and physical recovery. Seek help when the dreams, flashbacks and sleeplessness are ruining your daily life. Do not continue counseling with a judgmental counselor or minister who is unable to affirm the necessity and justifiability of your defensive choices, at a time when you most need confirmation of your own decency. There are experienced counselors who specialize in helping defense shooting survivors. Ask for professionals' names from the firearms instructors who trained you, or ask the mental health association for referral to a counselor with experience in post-traumatic stress disorder (PTSD).

One of the best sources of relief is peer counseling, time spent with others who have survived a traumatic event and dealt with the aftereffects. This is a two-pronged resource, offering comfort for those in crisis and an outreach for those who have survived and want to help others do the same. Most cities have rape crisis hot lines and support groups for women in crisis and constantly need volunteers. When you are ready, contact one of these groups and volunteer to help. The YWCA is a good starting place. If they don't have a women's crisis program in place, the staff may be able refer you to a women's organization that will welcome your help.

Strength from Adversity

Survivors of self-defense shootings are forever changed. Massad Ayoob compares the changes to scar tissue: for those able to grow from their experience, the trauma leaves behind a stronger character. Police officer Steve Chaney, featured in a segment of *Ultimate Survivors*, relates his feelings after surviving a second line-of-duty shooting. At first he wondered, "Why me?" Then he realized he was still alive and uninjured. "Some of life's positive lessons are not learned in positive ways," he tells viewers.[1]

Ultimately, only the survivor can make the decision how an attack will affect the rest of her life. We see people who go on to define their outlook and their entire life based on the experience of being a victim. This is tragic. While the survivor's life is forever altered, the goal of emotional and psychological recovery is to grow beyond the incident, becoming stronger and more resilient through the experience of recovery.

Notes

[1] Ultimate Survivors, Calibre Press, Inc., www.calibrepress.com, 800-323-0037.

CHAPTER 6

The Comfort of Home Safety

Personal safety literally begins at home. This requires an investment in safe living quarters, assuring the road-worthiness of your car, and budgeting for self-defense equipment and training despite all the other demands on your budget.

When you look for a new home or apartment, study the security provisions and see if you can identify potential danger spots. Every house's and each apartment's layout differs. Use your survival awareness to identify the weak points. If renting, the presence or absence of dead-bolt locks and window bars gives you a measure of the owner's commitment to tenant security. Most municipal codes require landlords to provide dead-bolt locks on doors, not just keyed doorknobs. Demand bars on ground-level windows or lease an apartment without ground-level access to windows or doors. If the landlord objects when you ask why these security devices are absent, look for another place to rent!

This is the first principle of home defense: If your home can be breached so easily and rapidly that you must be able to make an

Though the landscaping is attractive, these smart homeowners chose short, thin plantings, so there is no concealment in the yard, especially near this vulnerable basement window.

instantaneous response to danger, the problem does not hinge on the speed of your response. The problem lies in how to strengthen the perimeter of safety around your home! In other words, *home safety begins outside the home*, not inside it. If you feel you are unable to provide safe housing, reassess your personal priorities and analyze your commitment to your safety and well-being.

It is easy to equate a fenced yard with security, yet the common privacy fence serves primarily as a vision barrier and is as much a danger as an asset. Most residential fences can be broken through or leapt over, and once an intruder is concealed behind the fence, he can break into the house without worrying that anyone will report his crime. If deterrence is part of the fence's reason for existing, at least replace the common gate latches with a good lock so an intruder can't waltz right in at will. A neighbor is more likely to report someone breaking out a board in your fence or jumping over than he would someone who walks up the drive and opens your gate, as would a family member or utility worker.

Think twice before landscaping with a thick hedge or bushes that provide hiding places around the home. Thorny ornamental bushes positioned beneath windows and decks to discourage unwanted visitors are, of course, a reasonable exception.

An absolute requirement for home safety is bright, well-placed lighting. Home security lighting systems range from gimmicky to great. Consult the experts, yet maintain a skeptical attitude to select the most useful. At a minimum be sure your doorways, sidewalks, garage and halls are well lit. If you park in a garage, either leave a light on when you depart, or install lighting you can switch on by remote control before you enter.

While living near downtown Seattle some years ago, I narrowly avoided a prowler revealed by the light above the door. It was late when I approached the building door. As I drew within 20 feet, I saw a figure slip from the shadows, through the light's beam, then stop in the shadows between the building and an adjacent garage. Had I not detected movement, I would have been in easy striking distance while unlocking the door. I don't know if that prowler meant any harm, because I didn't stay around long enough to find out. His furtive actions indicated his that presence was not authorized. I hurried to another entrance, shaken by how easily I might have walked into danger had I approached a second later.

Install motion-activated lights around the home's exterior, not forgetting areas into which you cannot easily see. Sudden, bright illumination of the less visible parts of home and yard may convey the impression that an occupant of the home has detected a lurker's presence.

Create the illusion of an occupied home. During daytime hours, drawn shades indicate an empty home nearly as emphatically as windows revealing empty rooms. Instead, hang sheer draperies with sufficient texture and weight to occlude the view from outside, while still allowing daylight into the room. Buy and set timers to unpredictable intervals. For example, one timer might turn on the bathroom light for a

Simple motion activated light fixtures are easy to install and add a layer of safety.

few minutes in the middle of each night, as suggested by Tanya Metaksa in her excellent book Safe, *Not Sorry*.[1] A TV or radio playing for periods of time, lamps lit then extinguished, all cycling at varied hours of the day while you are absent, can discourage daytime burglaries.

The Inside Story

The value of a good-quality security alarm should not be underestimated. Remember, however, that even the best alarms incorporate a loud exterior siren or bells that alert you and your neighborhood of a break-in. They also serve to tell the intruder that his time is short. Make sure that your alarm system is installed by a reputable dealer and that the phone lines through which it operates are secure.

Even if you choose to install a security system, a number of secondary and companion safety provisions are necessary. First, consider the locks and keys barring intruders from your home. Re-key or change all locks when you move into a new home, whether as buyer or tenant. It is ridiculously easy for an intruder to obtain a key from a previous occupant.

Keys can be easily copied, which brings us to an important point: *separate your keys from anything that gives your address or telephone number*. If possible, keys should be carried in hand or on your person, not in a purse, which a purse-snatcher may target. Separate house keys from car keys, which can end up on a mechanic's clip board, in the hands of a valet, and other unsecured places. At work, don't leave your keys unattended on top of your desk, in your coat pocket or other vulnerable spots. Children who carry house keys must be capable of similar responsibilities.

The locks are as important as the keys they fit. Doors and windows need locks of sufficient strength to impede a burglar. Consider how an intruder might gain entrance to your home. All exterior home entrances should have metallic or solid-core doors – not ones with hollow or thin panels – fitted with dead-bolt locks. Bolts must reach over an inch into the door frame after passing through the strike plate shield. Long strike plate screws need to tap deeply into the door frame studs to secure it to the frame, and for greater kick-proofing, consider switching to a metal reinforced door frame.

Exterior doors generally open inward. If they open outward, be sure the hinges are not installed on the outside, where anyone can pop out the pins and lift the entire door off its hinges, thus gaining easy access to the home. Windows need sturdy metal or heavy wood frames, also fitted with locks. Take special care to secure basement and garage windows, where distance from the living area may mask the noise of an intruder breaking in.

While considering locks on doors and windows, don't forget attached garages. Here, the easiest unauthorized entry is from the roll-up door, which may be pushed up or even activated by an automatic garage door opener set to the factory default setting. If you use a remote garage door opener, reprogram it to a code of your own choice.

Sturdy, well-installed locks are one of the best values in which you can invest to shore up your home's defenses, whether you live in a century-old farm house or a new home in a subdivision.

(Your owner's manual will tell usually you how to do this. If it doesn't, contact a reputable garage door installer for advice.) In addition, block the garage door roller from being thrust up in the roller track by threading a padlock or a pin through a hole above the roller, or using some other device like a clamp to keep the door from being opened. Don't ignore the service door between attached garages and your home. It must be sturdy and fitted with a good lock.

Vertical sliding windows, especially in older wood frames, can be made more secure by adding a removable 1"x2" stick the height of the movable window pane to brace it shut. After several break-ins at an old apartment building where I once lived, the police told us that the burglars were inserting a wedge of wood or metal at the base of the window frame, then depressing the wedge to create enough leverage to break out the lock at the top of the old, wooden window frame. There was no noise of shattering glass, only the dull, wooden pop as the lock broke free of the frame. Be wary of doors with glass windows that, if broken, give access to the knob inside and the lock. If you choose not to replace this type of door, at least change the lock to the double-keyed, double-cylinder variety to keep a burglar from simply breaking out the small panes of glass and reaching through to turn the deadbolt knob on the inside.

If cursed with a double sliding glass door, better advice than the dowel in the lower track is placing a tension bar (like a chin-up exercise bar) midway between floor and top of the frame. If able, eliminate the sliding door altogether, because even the tension bar does nothing to prevent a burglar from smashing the glass or from lifting the door off its track and removing it altogether.

Finally, none of these precautions have much worth if doors and windows are left unsecured. After an Edmonds, Washington, woman survived a rape, then got to her gun and held the serial rapist for police, another local woman remarked to television reporters: "I'm so

A neatly trimmed 2x4 blocks this vulnerable floor-level window, adding security to the flimsy latch these kinds of windows usually have.

glad they caught him. It's getting warm and I need to be able to leave my sliding patio door open again." In hot weather, intruders often find houses open and waiting for them.

This is not a new problem. Richard Ramirez, known as the Night Stalker, found easy entry to dozens of homes during his 1984 reign of terror. An exceptionally hot California summer in which people found it impossible to keep windows and doors closed and locked gave him the opening he needed. All of his murders, rapes and torture took place inside the victims' homes, with entry made through open or poorly secured windows, sliding glass doors, garages and even pet doors.

Lock up your home before leaving, whether going on a five-minute errand to the store or going to work. An empty house with open windows is quite an invitation to those who would take your possessions or pounce on you when you return. If I return to an empty house, I pause after opening the car door and again at the front door to gather sensory impressions to see if anything is awry. If you have pets that customarily meet you at the door, their absence or demeanor can be a useful indicator. Stop and listen as you light the house; be aware of and cautiously inspect places where intruders might be concealed. Coat closets can be made safer by storing enough stuff on the floors that there is no room for an intruder to hide without moving some objects out of the closet.

While you are awake and alert at home, open doors and windows require an elevated level of awareness. If you lapse into Condition White – asleep, in the shower or pursuing other activities that decrease awareness – you need to secure doors and windows that are accessible from the ground. One of my friends admits that when she reads a good book, she becomes so absorbed in the story that activity around her really does not register. Aware of this tendency, she is careful where she indulges in her enjoyment of good literature.

A watchdog is a valuable addition to home security, primarily as a search partner, as an early warning device and as an excellent deterrent. If your pooch faithfully greets you whenever you return home, its absence might be the first warning of danger. Don't put too much trust in a dog's ability to overpower intruders, however. One quiet .22 bullet in the head removes a canine obstacle all too easily.

Finally, let me emphasize the importance of not entering a house you believe has been breached by an intruder. Police know that house

Though involved in the mundane task of folding clean laundry, Laurisa is armed and prepared to defend daughter Katie and herself, if the unexpected happens.

clearing is one of the most dangerous jobs imaginable. Although it is your "home turf," intruders have the upper hand because they command the element of surprise and can choose a tactically superior place in which to wait for you. You don't know where they are, if they are armed, or how many have intruded. Even if you immobilize one intruder, will you survive attacks by others backing up the one you stopped?

Again: if you find your home has been broken into, don't enter the house. Go elsewhere and call law enforcement officers who can search with trained dogs and other appropriate equipment while you wait outside in safety. This is one service your taxes buy.

Are You Safe Inside?

It's easy to feel safe and let down our guard once we're inside the front door. Even with the doors locked and blinds drawn, recognizing a predatory approach, whether over the phone, a mail solicitation or a caller at the door, can save a world of heartbreak.

Never tell anyone at the door or on the phone that you're alone. If a caller insists he must "talk to the man of the house," hang up or stage a fictional exchange in which the "man" refuses to come to the phone. Train family members, especially children, never to tell a caller who is home and who is out, when they'll return and how long they've been gone. Rapists and burglars use the telephone to gather information.

Any unidentified caller at the door should be treated with suspicion. First, remember that you are under no obligation to open the door for anyone. A common home invasion ploy uses a nicely dressed female accomplice, who knocks on the door. Lulled by the idea that the stranger is "just a woman," the occupant opens the door to find the woman plus one or more men who force their way inside. Multiple intruders are common in gang-committed crimes. Be extremely guarded in opening your door to any stranger, and if you choose to own a gun for self defense have it on your person. Otherwise, the hope of fending off this crime is very limited.

Several useful door blocking devices are available, including Frank Hilliard's Lit'l Surprise, which uses a sturdy steel rod to block the door from the inside when you must open it to unknown callers but which is easily removed when family members are in and out of the house.

Criminals may also disguise themselves as repair or utility workers. This kind of contact should be by prior appointment only. If you are uncertain if these are legitimate workers, don't automatically let them inside. Take extra steps to verify their bona fides. Request company identification and verify the credentials with the utility company, your landlord or whoever sent the individual before letting them into your home. Leave the worker standing on the porch with the door locked

She's got her hands full dealing with one burglar, and is not yet aware of the accomplice coming from another room. House clearing is better left to the professionals!

while you get your concealed weapon, if necessary. Once inside, monitor them while they perform their work. Have your firearm or self-defense weapon on your person. If at any time their words or actions make you feel threatened or uneasy, tell them to leave. If they resist, you may have to escape and call the police from elsewhere, so easy access to wallet, cell phone and keys makes good sense.

A lone woman knocking at the door may be a decoy for a hidden accomplice.

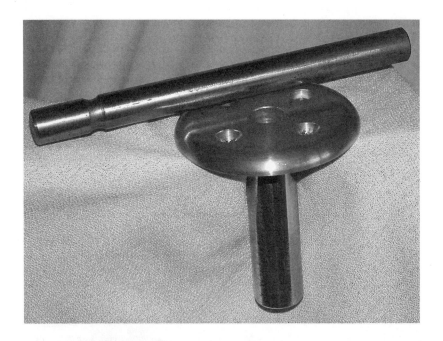

This low-tech door blocker is sunk in a small hole drilled in the floor, while the sturdy steel rod is removable so it can be set aside when you are not inside the house.

I repeat, you are under NO obligation to allow into your home anyone with whom you do not feel safe and comfortable. This includes ex-husbands, former boyfriends, distant relations, anyone from your job or casual acquaintances. YOU control the access to your home. Children's visitors must also meet with your approval and children should be trained never to invite anyone inside without parental approval.

There is much we can do to increase home security. Some of it costs nothing, requiring only behavioral changes, though sometimes those are the most challenging! Take a few minutes and consider how you would break into your house if you were a burglar. Look for vulnerable entrance points, then set about to strengthen them.

Notes

[1] Safe, not sorry, op. cit.

When an unexpected caller knocks at the door, Laurisa asks her daughter Katie to step back into another room, as she uses the peep hole to decide whether to open the door.

CHAPTER 7

The Bump in the Night

"**W**hat was that?!"

Have you ever been wakened from sound sleep by a shattering or bumping noise? Most of us have had this unnerving experience. You awake and try to determine the source of the noise. Is it merely your four-year-old trying to get a drink of water, a pet scratching at the door, or an intruder who has gotten inside?

This is one defense scenario in which immediate action is inadvisable. Even if someone has unlawfully entered your house, there are many reasons not to immediately seek out and attack the intruder. First, is it really a criminal? Could an innocent person be in your home without your knowledge? Do your teenagers have friends they might allow to come in and sleep off too much beer? Do any friends, relatives or other innocent people have keys to your home? In such circumstances, a "wait and see" approach is advisable.

Use Your Phone!

If you are certain that ominous noises are not caused by family members or welcome guests and you're convinced that an intruder is inside, go to a pre-established tactical headquarters or safe room and dial 911 or another emergency number. When you call, give the police dispatcher information along these lines:

"There is an intruder in my home at 100 Center Street. I think he's on the first floor. I will wait on the second floor. I am a white female, 5'5" and have on a red bathrobe. I am armed with a snub-nosed revolver. I repeat, there is an intruder in my home at. . . ."

State your address first, then describe the situation and give pertinent details. Do not rely on enhanced 911 to identify the address from which your call originates. Make the message brief and to the point, then repeat the information. Experts advise you to stay on the line with the emergency dispatcher so you can identify the responding officers. Locked in a safe area of your home, it is wise to refuse entry to anyone you cannot positively identify as a law enforcement officer. Every self-defense situation is unique in itself, and you will have to remain fluid and able to make decisions based on the circumstances. If it becomes necessary to defend yourself or family members from the intruder, you may have to break off communications with the dispatcher or flee the room.

Why offer your personal description and reveal that you are armed? Two reasons. One: the personal description is vital because you may be mistaken for a burglar yourself when the police arrive. Two: law enforcement agencies will respond more rapidly to a scene where they know at least one firearm is involved. The presence of a deadly weapon tells them this is an explosive situation.

After calling for help, you have two choices. You can remain silently ensconced in your safe room, taking cover behind a bullet-stopping obstacle, weapon in hand so long as it is apparent the intruder is not getting any closer to the area in which you are sheltering. Pause a moment and listen again for noises that may reveal the intruder's location. Contrary to the movies, no one can move through unfamiliar territory without creating noises. As an alternative, you may choose to warn the burglar: "Hey, whoever you are! The police have been called and are on their way. We are armed. Leave the house immediately and we will not harm you!" In any event, do not abandon your room's security unless the safety of children or other dependents is threatened.

Evan Marshall suggests a more direct approach. His version of the challenge is simply, "Get out!" delivered in command voice. He strongly recommends arranging the home so the defender can wait, firearm in hand, at the head of a stairwell or a hall, blocking access to the rest of the family.

The problems with seeking out and confronting a housebreaker are many. He is running the game and you will likely be at his mercy. Your safety is greatly enhanced if you can take refuge in a secure area, call for help and wait out the intrusion from a protected position.

The Safe Room

I've previously referred to a "safe room." Simply put, this is a "hardened" area containing emergency equipment such as weapons, a cell phone, flashlights and other necessities. When you come home, go straight to your safe room and place your wallet or purse, keys and wireless phone in the same place each time. This may be the best place for the cell phone's charger, to be sure it will be fully powered if ever needed in an emergency.

Alternate escape routes from the safe room are advisable in the case of arson or other dangers. This may require getting a fire escape chain ladder if your safe room is not on the ground floor. Alternatively, you may need to leave your safe room to ensure your dependents' safety. Call the police, and then pad quietly from room to room, gathering up the smaller children. Wake the older children with the instruction to remain exactly where they are and lock them safely in their rooms, unless you believe the intruder may gain access to that child's room.

Other times, the emergency may make it necessary to secure the safety of family members while calling the authorities, and it is in these moments that wireless communication is worth every expensive cent it costs.

In a two-story home, if all the bedrooms are on the upper floor, you may choose to establish a place of strategic dominance at the head of the stairs. This denies an intruder any access to the vulnerable sleeping areas so that he must come through your gunfire before he can reach those in your care. Know what lies beyond the area into which you may shoot, and plan accordingly. If possible add furnishings that can double as cover behind which you can take shelter while preventing further intrusion.

In "hardening" a safe room, replace the door with a solid-core or steel door fitted with a good dead-bolt lock. In addition, a quick-access gun safe might be an appropriate accessory, as would be a bright flashlight, body armor, and some kind of furnishing that provides cover and protection from an assailant's gunfire. You might want to stash first-aid supplies, with emphasis on dressings to staunch blood flow, in this area along with any creature comforts you may need if facing a prolonged wait.

The Importance of Practice

How strange it is that we practice musical skills and our tennis game, yet we rarely practice self defense scenarios!

A sample exercise is surveying your house or apartment, as suggested at the end of the last chapter. Starting at your car or front door, enter, looking carefully for all the spots where an assailant might hide. You may decide to install better lighting, move or trim certain bushes, or clear out boxes and debris in your garage that could conceal assailants. Entering your home, check for alcoves or closets where an assailant might hide. Check for fast access to light switches, or the consider changing to remote controlled lighting.

Moving through your home, be aware of heavy furniture that

Ingenuity and proper equipment gives this mom and her son an alternative escape route in case of home intrusion or other dangers on their rural homestead.

During a practice session, Mom leads the way, showing her son how to safely get from the home's upper story on to the fire ladder.

would provide you cover in a gunfight, and look for places where an assailant might conceal himself. You might choose to relocate a large, packed bookshelf to a strategic position where it could provide bullet-stopping cover. Consider rearranging furniture to impede unauthorized entry through a window or sliding glass door. You should be sure the location of a waterbed or a large, packed chest of drawers provides bullet-stopping cover in your safe room. Crouch or lie down behind the furniture to be sure it is large enough to protect your body.

After some urging from his mom, the boy follows.

Successful practice earns a hug and words of praise. This mom enjoys more peace of mind, knowing she and her son are prepared to face a variety of emergencies that may require leaving the house from the upper story.

Families with children should assign bedrooms so the armed adults can protect the dependents. Take the room at the head of the hallway or assign the children to upstairs bedrooms, if the sleeping rooms are located on both first and second floors. Work out a home-defense plan with other adults who share the house and brief youngsters about what to expect in an emergency. This is also a good time to go over escaping fires, gas leaks and other dangers.

Another exercise that can be conducted with a bit more levity is one suggested by Massad Ayoob in his excellent book, *In the Gravest Extreme.*[1] He recommends playing a game of hide-and-seek with your children. They know all the best hiding places, and as he says, any place your four-foot child can hide offers concealment to a motivated, full-size housebreaker.

For renters, apartment halls and doorways are excellent places to practice your survival awareness. How many times have you rounded a corner in a public hallway, in the grip of a daydream or a worry, and gasped as you almost collided with a neighbor? Learn not to walk carelessly around blind corners or and know who else is in apartment house laundry rooms or utility rooms before you enter. Cut a wide path around 90° corners, open doors fully and look in before entering. Make the most of these utilitarian moments as practice to sharpen your awareness of clues like noise, movement, smell and shadow, developing skills that may someday alert you to an assailant's presence before you are in his grasp.

Your safety depends on knowing who occupies a public space such as an elevator or laundry room before you commit yourself to entering. Learn by daily practice to scan the room, including behind the door you just opened, to ascertain if another person is present. A door that opens against a wall can simply be pushed until it bangs into the wall or door stop to check for anyone hiding behind it.

Information Control

Just as you guard access to your home and its occupants, it is prudent to limit publicly available information about yourself. Using initials instead of your full name on the mailbox, telephone directory or other listings helps protect you from people who target women. Don't use Ms., Mrs., or Miss or any thing else that indicates gender. When asked for a phone number by a sales clerk accepting your check, give a false number, a ruse suggested by Paxton Quigley, author of *Armed and Female*[2]. Even if the clerk seems harmless, a member of the store staff or another shopper may divert that information to harass you. Never reveal your home address, telephone numbers, birth date and especially your social security number.

Businesswomen who need to give clients contact information are safer renting an offsite mail box and phone service. Never list residential telephones or home addresses on business cards or promotional literature that you hand out. Even if you are careful to whom you give your card, you cannot control where it goes after it is out of your hands.

A rich resource for thieves is the information deposited in the garbage can. Paper shredders are quite affordable, or set aside one trash can for "burnables" if you have a fireplace or woodstove in which to destroy credit card slips, offers of credit, or any other paper containing personal data. Be particularly careful what you leave in the trash in a motel room or other place outside the home. Exercise caution when communicating or doing business over the internet. Be extremely guarded in revealing any personal information, and monitor children's on-line activity for the same exposure.

Earlier we discussed protecting the security of your keys. Along the same line of thought, the information you carry in an easily snatched purse can lead a committed criminal to your door. One of my friends

An intruder can stuff himself into a surprisingly small hiding place, given enough time and motivation.

has solved this problem by carrying identification, licenses, emergency cash, credit cards and even a spare key in a separate business card case like those found in office-supply stores. The case is small enough to carry inside her pocket where it is less vulnerable to theft.

Call Me Crazy, but –

Do the preparations in this chapter sound a little paranoid? They're not! There is a big difference between a fear-ridden person and one who acknowledges the possibility of danger and practices simple precautions to prevent it. The Department of Justice reports that nearly 15% of all crimes of violence take place in the victim's home, and another 15% occur near the home.[3] Violent crime is not always something that happens to other people!

Notes

[1] Ayoob, In the Gravest Extreme, op. cit.

[2] Quigley, Paxton, *Armed and Female*, released in paperback in 1990 by St. Martin's Press, 175 5th Ave., New York, NY 10010.

[3] http://www.ojp.usdoj.gov/bjs/abstract/cvusst.htm, op. cit.

CHAPTER 8

Campus Safety for Young Adults

The morbid focus placed on school shootings in recent years has nearly eclipsed all the other crimes to which American students are subjected. And while shooters on campuses far too frequently take the lives of others without facing any real resistance before they kill themselves or in the minority of cases are stopped by other means, students are astronomically more likely to fall prey to the crimes of aggravated assault, robbery and forcible rape.

What defenses are available to students, especially at the collegiate level, where they are entering early adulthood yet are part of the controlled society so prevalent in academia? Not only are firearms prohibited on most campuses, even less than lethal devices like the Taser® are usually restricted as well. Consider the irony: in this supposedly life-preparatory setting, many safety preparations are pre-empted by the school, and in the case of state-run schools, by the very state itself. And yet we expect graduates to emerge ready to take their place in society!

In a fit of national blindness, we seem to think that college campuses cocoon their students in a safe environment. Unfortunately, that's not the case. In 2006, 2,802 students were victims of violent crime on American campuses and 506 cases of forcible rape were reported. If a student is sufficiently mature to be sent away from home for higher education, she must be taught how to avoid becoming the victim of violent crime, as well as being ready to practice prevention methods and physical self-defense. Without those skills, her place in the crime statistics compiled on the Security On Campus website[1] is nearly assured.

Campus Crime Prevention

Certainly some schools are statistically safer than others, and the U.S. Department of Education tabulates and makes college campus crime statistics available online[2]. Still, even campuses that take active countermeasures such as keycard entries, video surveillance, strict substance abuse policies and rigid parent notification procedures are not free of crime.

Dormitories and open campuses must look like a rich resource to human predators! In suburban neighborhoods, a predator has to deal with alarmed homes, neighborhood watch, and other deterrents. On campuses, not only are there people moving around at all hours of day and night, but while the main dorm door may be locked and alarmed, one may see ground-floor windows hanging open, whether the room's occupant is inside or has forgotten to lock up when she left for class. Once inside the dorm, the predator can move beyond the room he has accessed and do his damage, if he finds that room does not contain what he wants.

Outside their lodgings, students traveling solo or two-by-two look like easy prey, so girls are encouraged to go in groups whenever possible. Other activity that makes the criminals' jobs easier comes when students leave late-night parties, or fall under the influence of alcohol or drugs. These students are easy targets for opportunistic criminals, including other students. Attacks also occur at parties, when young women are sexually assaulted by several fellow partiers, or suffer date rape after going into a secluded area with the assailant on any number of plausible excuses.

Preventing these crimes requires abstinence from intoxicants, as well as knowing how to put up an aggressive physical defense. Training like Tony Blauer's *Personal Defense Readiness*[3] programs should be a prerequisite for leaving home and going away to school!

Students Cooperate to Stay Safe

When I asked about campus safety issues, Stephanie Beamer, director of an all-women's cooperative house at Oregon State University, told me about a number of student safety programs in place at OSU: "When growing up we had people looking out for us and people to take us places, whereas a campus environment is very different and new and unknown. Still, I think it's assumed that women know how to protect themselves," she explains. Some women carry pepper spray, she reported, and a few carry knives.

Women walking alone causes the most concern, and often friends who are driving will give a friend a ride home, even if it is only for two or three blocks. Most of the young women Stephanie knows choose to drive to their destination if they can't find people who will walk with them. In addition, a student-operated transportation system is funded through student tuition making a van available to pick up students and take them to their destination safely. The campus is equipped with emergency telephones that are directly connected to the public safety department. Students on campuses so equipped should take note of the location of the phones and make that part of their awareness, though an organized predator may find these easy to disable. Once again, a cell phone is a good idea, if not an out-and-out necessity.

Stephanie believes that most female students understand the dangers of walking alone, and they are encouraged to tell someone where they are going and when they expect to return before heading out. One OSU safety initiative formed a list of male students who were willing to be on-call for students needing a safe escort. Most of the concern is over night time excursions, Stephanie commented, but she noted that one of the worst abductions in Corvallis, Oregon – home of OSU – occurred in broad daylight when a visiting college student was abducted while doing some cleaning outside the apartments her sister and brother-in-law operated on the edge of the campus.

On campus, male students receive information on sexual assault in addition to the rape prevention training offered for the women. Young men are encouraged to move beyond simply being bystanders while a woman is at risk or being assaulted, Stephanie told me. "I personally believe that it is extremely intertwined with women's safety; males need to be involved for this issue to be resolved," she emphasizes.

Surviving Campus Shootings

Though the incidents of death or injury from campus shootings are far smaller in number than other violent crime, we would be remiss if we failed to suggest strategies for surviving these atrocities. One of the biggest advantages the campus shooter enjoys is a field of victims who

Unfortunately, this girl is easy pickings for criminals who need to avoid witnesses.

Without the buffering safety of crowds, this student chooses her walking route carefully, is alert to her surroundings, and wastes no time getting to her destination.

are not only unable to fight back on his terms, but who are also usually stunned into submission. At a minimum, we must guide our students through the mental preparation to increase their odds of survival.

Campus shooters are usually somehow disgruntled, whether from social abuse, failing to receive academic advancement, being dismissed from the school, or breaking off a romantic relationship. Many have often expressed their despondency verbally before violently acting out their distress. Studies show that many school shooters stated their intentions before the incident but were not taken seriously by their peers.

In a few noteworthy cases, students have stopped the killer's attack, as in the 2002 shooting at the Appalachian School of Law; the Paducah, Kentucky school shooting; and the Kinkel shooting in Springfield, Oregon. In other cases, staff stopped the shooting, like the teacher who stopped Barry Loukaitis in Moses Lake, Washington; the assistant principal who stopped the Pearl, Mississippi shooter; and the banquet hall owner who disarmed the teen who shot up the eighth-grade dance in Edinboro, Pennsylvania in 1998.

Responsible parents make sure their young women know how to defeat common attacks with more than just desperate, helpless flailing, as McKenzie first demonstrates at the beginning of a practice session with her mom.

Brady explains to her daughter how the thumbs of the grabbing hands are most easily overcome, should someone grab and attempt to pull her where she does not wish to go.

These courageous acts are also extremely dangerous, and, of course, cannot be recommended without qualification. Still, had more of the victims understood how guns work and acknowledged the ultimate responsibility they bore for their own survival, the tables might have been turned on school shooters who pause to reload.

Instead of just blindly believing that the school administration is responsible for student safety, students need to memorize the routes of escape in the varied classrooms, lecture halls, and other school facilities. When classroom seating is not assigned, a seat close to a door is a good idea; in libraries, cafeterias, and other public areas, choose a seat that accommodates easy exit. A rapid escape or exit alternative is probably the student's best choice, and preparation to do that requires acknowledgement that this kind of danger could present itself in their classroom, as well as prior examination out of the various areas they frequent. If the student shows no interest in making this survey, a wise parent should accompany them on a walk around the school facility and point out how to get away from various areas.

Too often we deny that anything is wrong when there are reasonably clear clues that an attack is about to happen. Do not hesitate to leave the classroom or go and stand near a doorway if a student becomes agitated. Young people hate to stand out from a crowd, and all to often stay in the flock as it is headed for slaughter. The all-too-human tendency to stand and gape as someone suffers an emotional meltdown should be resisted. *The safest response is to leave such scenes immediately.*

Following her mom's instructions, McKenzie discovers how easily she can break free of a hard, two-handed grab.

Brady spars with her daughter, practicing escapes from a grab coming from behind. Taught and practiced efficiently at home, these lifesaving skills are essential for young women in today's world. Kudos to the smart parents preparing their daughter for life's realities!

You Are Responsible for Yourself!

One of the biggest lessons to come with adulthood is that the individual is responsible for what she does, and that she must prevent harmful things that others would do to her. Whether this entails standing up and getting away to a safer place when another student is violently acting out, or whether it is dealing forcefully with an overaggressive date, or maybe it means telling someone who always seems to be shadowing you, to go away and quit following you, all these assertive actions contribute to personal safety when practiced alongside other sensible crime prevention steps.

Personal safety requires good advance planning. Completing a safe late-night study session may require checking materials out of the library early in the evening so that cramming can be done in the safety of your dorm room or sorority house, thus avoiding a midnight trip home from the library. Order in meals rather than making a midnight trek to the all-night burger joint, or better yet, anticipate the need for a meal in advance and buy food beforehand.

This kind of strategic thinking is the mark of a young woman who is ready to be out on her own. Parents need to teach and reward their daughters for this kind of responsibility.

Notes

[1] Security On Campus, Inc., 133 Ivy Lane, Suite 200, King Of Prussia, PA 19406, 888-251-7959 http://www.security-oncampus.org/

[2] http://www.ope.ed.gov/security/Search.asp

CHAPTER 9

Personal Safety at Work

"Workplace violence" is a buzzword that human resources managers dread and a condition that continues to plague American workers. The Department of Labor's 2005 Survey of Workplace Violence Prevention estimated that fully 70% of the businesses surveyed had no concrete plan for preventing attacks on their workers.[1] Women are the targets of more than half of all nonfatal workplace assaults, and are more likely than men to be attacked by someone they know: a coworker, repeat customer, patient or domestic partner.

In 2002, the Occupational and Safety and Health Administration (OSHA) estimated that two million Americans had been victims of workplace violence[2]. A year earlier, the Department of Justice estimated that 1.3 million simple assaults, 325,000 aggravated assaults, 36,500 rapes and sexual assaults, 70,000 robberies and 900 homicides occurred yearly in the workplace. As with all statistics, the numbers quoted vary wildly: the U.S. Department of Labor reported that in private industry alone there were 441 on-the-job homicides in 2006.

While massacres committed by disgruntled workers captivate the news media, the daily dangers to working women are more prevalent and considerably broader in scope than these sensational crimes. The hazards women face daily go largely unreported in the press, being less dramatic than a madman shooting up a factory. Because threats to personal safety can never be completely removed, you remain responsible for your own protection at work.

Making Choices

James Potter, workplace violence prevention consultant, identifies denial of personal vulnerability as contributing to the continuation of unsafe conditions. "We seem to accept any decrease in violence stats as a victory, with no outrage about how high the occurrence totals still are. We've slowly become calloused to this high level of personal violence happening all around us," Potter notes. "Do we demand that someone find ways to preempt more of this personal terrorism all about us? Or, is it time to take responsibility for our own well-being by learning self-safekeeping that works, anyplace, at any time?" he asks.

An employer's failure to correct hazards is a good reason to seek a better position elsewhere! When considering a new job, carefully study the risks the job and location entail. During a job search, pros and cons weighed against different offers should absolutely consider safety and self-defense issues just as seriously as the salary. Job seekers would do well to investigate the employers' commitment to workplace safety. Start by just keeping your eyes and ears attuned to the environment during your job interview. Does the building entrance have good visibility and is the approach free of heavy foliage or other concealment? Are security cameras or concave mirrors installed in and around the building? Are the windows plastered with signs and advertisements behind which a robbery could occur undetected? Are drop safes or time access safes used to secure cash? Considerations such as these are particularly important in "high risk" occupations such as clerking at an all-night convenience store.

Study the location of the business and any neighborhoods to which you may be required to travel. Consider the safety of the employee parking area and the walk from it into the workplace. Observe customers and workers, watching for disrespectful or threatening language, racial or sexual insults or inappropriate physical contact.

Finally, the type of work sought influences the statistical chance that you will be the target of workplace violence. Which workers are least protected?

The Forbes website reports that in 2002, homicide claimed the lives of 205 retail workers[3], well above the 50 police officers murdered on the job. The Bureau of Labor Statistics also underscores that retail sales workers are recurring targets, but the common notion that professionals are safer is fallacious: assaults against pharmacists, physicians, and nurses are common and sometimes end in murder. Supervisors and managers are also among higher risk categories, regardless of the business sector occupied.[4]

At elevated risk are workers filling shifts that fall between 9 p.m. to 6 a.m. In retail settings, clerks who work alone are particularly endangered, with hazards magnified by perils including a remote location, poor lighting, obscured windows, the absence of escape routes, and duties including stocking merchandise from, or dumping trash in, areas outside the relative protection of the well-lit or occupied portions of the store. A 2002 OSHA report identified workers who exchange money with the public, provide transportation, or have extensive contact with the public[5] as being at higher risk.

Understanding how and under what circumstances people are injured at work helps us focus on appropriate self-defense training and tools. In no way is shooting skill alone sufficient. Disarming skills against both gun and knife are recommended, as well as unarmed defenses to escape grabs, parry a blow, slip or defuse the power of a punch, and even verbal defenses.

Responses to Harassment

The old adage that "Words can never hurt me" is not completely true. In the workplace, verbal harassment and veiled threats are not only illegal but also often lead to physical symptoms of stress, anxiety and decreased work performance. Judith Weiss, a Texas-based self-

defense trainer and editor of the Assault Prevention Information
Network, gives a cogent description of worker harassment and the
challenge of choosing an appropriate response:

"Mini-rapes – the verbal and physical intrusions that women
routinely put up with – may be a simple attempt to demean and
demoralize us, or may be a test to see whether we are compliant or
easily manipulated (and therefore a likely rape victim). About 70%
of assaults on women are by people we know (dates, coworkers,
spouses, neighbors, family members) and occur where we live, work

*Kathy practices knife disarming skills to augment her skill at escapes from
grabs and other attacks.*

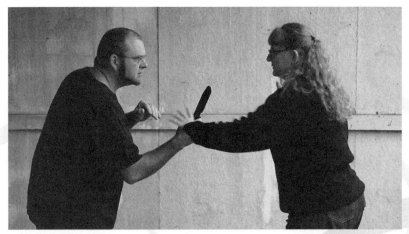

In a lightening-fast response, she puts her hand on Don's knife hand.

With both hands controlling the knife hand, Kathy is ready to apply a wrist lock.

Rolling his wrist over, Kathy effects release of the knife.

It's not necessarily over with the knife on the ground! Additional pressure further disrupts the attacker's balance and will put him over backwards, giving Kathy a better chance to escape unharmed.

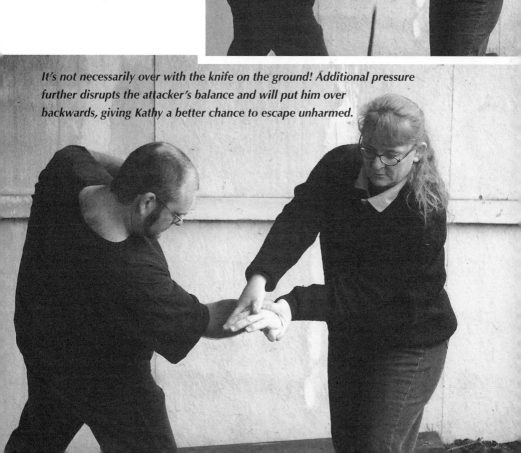

and socialize. . . . We do want to discourage or interrupt a verbal or physical intrusion, but if the perpetrator is not actually threatening bodily harm, it would be inappropriate (and probably illegal) to wound or kill him. . . .Verbal assertiveness and simple evasive techniques (like a release from a wrist grab) may be enough for pest control."

Assertive deterrence by verbal and physical deflection should be part of every woman's job skills. As discussed in earlier chapters, predators prefer easy prey and are less likely to harass the woman who early on and actively resists bullying or exploitation. Sadly, there are so many easier targets on which the harasser may prey.

Abuse in the workplace must be documented and reported, even if the employer refuses to take the complaints seriously. If your supervisor belittles or jokes about your complaint, document your report in writing and keep that record safe. Physically resisting an attack by a fellow-worker will be more defensible if you can prove you tried every other means available to you before the conflict escalated.

Even then, the amount of force used to stop undesired contact, groping, grabs, or more serious assault must be in proportion to the offense. In the following chapter, we discuss vital intermediate defenses and physical skills that have a very real application in fending off creeps, gropers and worse.

Coworker Problems

Along with worker-on-worker harassment, remain aware of fellow workers' backgrounds. Listening to your coworkers can alert you to personal conflicts that may migrate into the workplace. The Center for Disease Control estimates that homicide is the leading cause of death for women in the work place, and one-third of all homicides not associated with robbery or crimes by strangers are the result of intimate partner violence, according the University of Iowa Injury Prevention Research Center.[6]

If you worry someone you work with may become violent or be the target of aggression, you will need to choose the appropriate degree of

Physical defense skills include knowing what to do if a harasser grabs your arms or hands in a controlling manner.

Without harming her practice partner at all, Diane has slipped out of his grasp. In the workplace, this escape allows a woman to choose the kind of defensive response appropriate to the situation, be that harsh words, leaving the area or, if the attack, continues a physical defense.

intervention. At a minimum, being aware and monitoring workplace "time bombs" will give you an enormous advantage over most workers who are completely surprised when violence erupts and they are caught in the crossfire. Early recognition of behavioral cues, as well as learning techniques to prevent or diffuse volatile situations, is a useful first step that may prevent more serious dangers. Loren Christensen's book Surviving *Workplace Violence*[7] is an excellent source from which to learn the warning signs and what to do before, during and after a workplace assault.

Give wide berth to clients or coworkers displaying danger such as verbal threats against an employer, supervisor or coworkers; trouble accepting authority; obsessions about grudges; real or imagined romances or other troubled coworker relationships; social withdrawal; legal, financial or marital problems; inability to accept criticism or take responsibility for problems; substance abuse; recently disciplined or passed over for promotion; history of violent behavior; manifestations of despair or depression, paranoia, suspicions or jealousy; and mood swings.

Unless personally attacked, quickly leaving the scene of a dangerous confrontation involving a coworker lets you call for help instead of become a hostage or a victim. The layout of the work area can aid or interfere with your ability to scan for danger, as well as hinder escape during an attack. If you can, arrange your workspace for maximum visibility, with an especially good view of public entrances. When arranging your own personal work area, resist the urge to turn your back to the world, as many do to improve concentration. Your chair should face the entrance into your personal space.

In jobs or circumstances that entail elevated risk, seriously consider a deep or angled reception counter that offers greater protection. If that is not possible, rearrange generic workplace furnishings to limit physical accessibility to your person. Most importantly, know various escape routes, and be sure that back doors or other alternative routes are not blocked by trash, storage boxes or other detritus. A keyed deadbolt is not an appropriate lock for an emergency exit, of course, but especially in small businesses these kinds of oversights often go unnoticed until an emergency.

At a minimum, employers can be expected to provide a secure workplace with ID badges and limited access, good lighting, alarm systems, video surveillance, drop safes to minimize cash on hand, and equip offsite workers with cell phones, as well as putting workers on

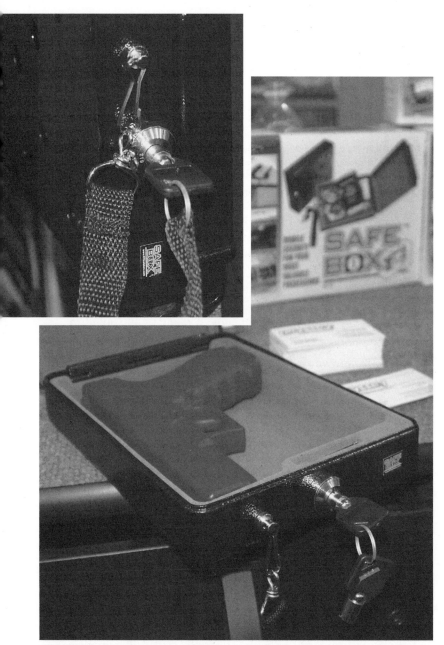

The Safe Box product uses a keyed lock and hardware to which the box attaches to protect a small gun from theft or tampering. If you choose to secure a gun in the work place, yet cannot carry it on your person, you must be sure you can lock the gun securely away from anyone but yourself.

a schedule with check points to keep supervisors informed of their location. When appropriate, use buddy systems, a security escort, or simply refuse to go to job sites where the client has exhibited violent responses.

With increasing frequency, carrying defensive tools is restricted in the workplace, as management struggles to understand and prevent violence. If prohibited from carrying a self-defense gun, pepper spray, knife or other weapon at work, you owe it to yourself to ratchet up your alertness, hone your unarmed skills and increase escape route awareness even more. A quick glance at your desk top will reveal items that can be improvised as weapons. Remember, though, if you can strike a blow with a tool or furnishing, so can an assailant.

Entrepreneurs and employees who are able to possess handguns and other weapons for defense at work may feel safe with the gun locked in the desk drawer. While a gun anywhere on the premises is better than none at all, I think it creates a false sense of security, especially for women who are at greater risk of a bare-handed attack. Concealing a handgun beneath business attire is challenging, yet it can be accomplished. Carry devices like Kramer Handgun Leather's Confidant® holster undershirt and elastic belly bands and thigh holsters, like those marketed by Galco provide deep concealment that keeps the gun on your person.[9] It is available to you when you go to the supply room, greet a client, and perform other duties that take you away from your desk.

Professional women have one of the more difficult dress codes to balance against sensibility and safety. Instead of one-piece dresses, skirted suits or pants suits will more easily conceal a small, defensive handgun carried at the waistline. For freedom of movement that facilitates defense or escape, consider trouser suits or wear pleated or fuller skirts. Instead of spike heels, acceptable low-heeled alternatives include dressy versions of the classic loafer or modifications of the ballet slipper. Accessories like neck scarves are not without risk, as are chains or jewelry that will not break away with a brisk tug.

Deep concealment devices like Kramer Handgun Leather's Confidant® (left) or the Smart Carry Invisible Holster (right) can conceal small guns beneath the typical business attire Jacqueline and the author wear.

A belly band, like this one by Galco can conceal a small gun like this 9mm Kahr PM9 when standards call for a dress.

Some find a thigh holster even better concealment for small guns, especially if their wardrobe contains a lot of dresses. This rig is made by Galco.

Flashy or expensive jewelry may also target you for a spur-of-the moment robbery, so we must recommend a conservative approach to accessories, too.

Tough Times All Over

In a study focused on health care worker's dangers, the National Security Institute accurately diagnosed one cause of dangers. "In the shrinking job market, employees feel they must prove themselves and devote more and more time to their careers. Employers struggle to keep companies productive and successful. Both employers and employees have need to be reminded that a safe, secure work environment enables both to achieve their goals."

Avoid personal work habits that increase your risk, including staying late at work, going in to work early or on weekends when the building is deserted, and failing to report harassment to management for fear it will effect your chances for promotion. All represent very real dangers, and you will gain little if you become unable to work due to death, injury or stress.

Notes

[1] Survey of Workplace Violence Prevention 2005: A special survey conducted by the Bureau of Labor Statistics, Department of Labor for the National Institute for Occupational Safety and Health, Centers for Disease Control and Prevention, Department of Health and Human Services, BLS Press Release, October 27th, 2006

[2] Occupational Safety and Health Administration Fact Sheet, 2002; and Bureau of Justice Statistics, 2001, Violence in the Workplace, 1993-1999. Washington, D.C., U.S. Department of Justice.

[3] http://www.forbes.com/2002/09/03/0903worksafe.html

[4] Occupational Safety and Health Administration Fact Sheet. Op cit.

[5] ibid.

[6] University of Iowa Injury Prevention Research Center. Feb. 2001. *Workplace Violence: A Report to the Nation.* Iowa City, IA.

7 *Surviving Workplace Violence* by Loren Christensen, ISBN 978-1-58160-465-8, Paladin Press, Gunbarrel Tech Center, 7077 Winchester Circle, Boulder, CO 80301, 303-443-7250 www.paladin-press.com

[8] Kramer Handgun Leather, P. O. Box 112154, Tacoma, WA 98411 or Smart Carry Invisible Holster, Concealed Protection 3, Inc., 940 – 7th St NW, Largo, FL 33770 www.smartcarry.com 888-459-2358

[9] Galco Gunleather, 2019 W Quail Ave., Phoenix, AZ 85027

CHAPTER 10

Hit 'em Where It Hurts

"**I** was asleep. He was on me so fast I didn't have time to do anything. Besides, he had a knife," confided the first woman. "He had my arms pinned down. I couldn't have used a gun even if I had one. All I could see was the Bible on the headboard of my bed, so I concentrated on it to keep my sanity while he raped me," another confided later.

I was at a women's exhibition promoting self defense and firearms classes with an aggressive sign that asked, "Could You Stop a Rapist?" Relating their stories, both women desperately needed to convince me – and themselves – that nothing could have prevented the rape they endured. Both spoke quietly for a few minutes, with obvious effort to dismiss the possibility that anything might have facilitated their escape. While I never question the decisions made by a sexual assault survivor, the conversations took the sunshine from my day. I felt sad that neither had detected the rapist entering the house or been able to fight back. I was more troubled that neither would consider preparing for the possibility of further danger and seemed to sadly accept their role as victim.

Since you've made it this far in the book, you know that I earnestly advocate crime avoidance over fighting, and escape over shooting. Safe housing, safe behavior, and awareness of danger when you're at home, work, in your car or in public, are among the first survival lessons I want to emphasize.

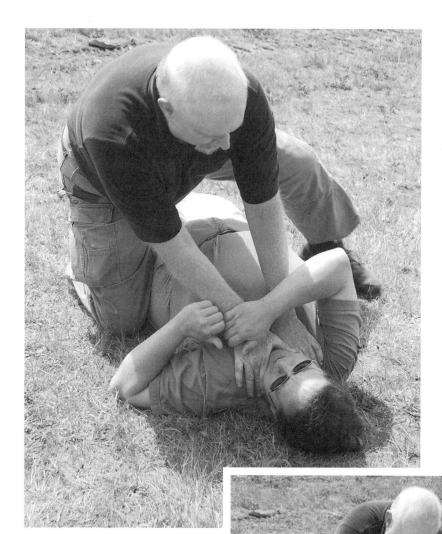

Think you're helpless if pinned down in a prone posture? Diane Walls shows the fallacy of that belief!

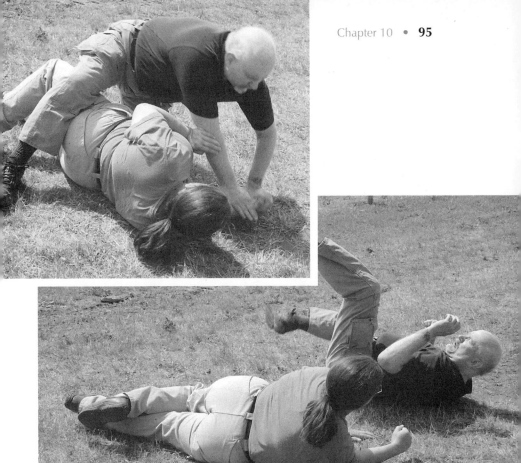

Although I believe that a gun can be a valuable asset – one that we'll discuss at length in later chapters – we need to realize that the gun is merely a safety rescue tool. A gun is of no help unless we are mentally prepared to fight back and know how to escape an assailant's restraint to gain the time to reach the weapon. Finally, the gun is inappropriate against a minor threat: even displaying a gun is justified only in situations where innocent life is in immediate danger. How much better it would be to avoid or deter the predator before suffering rape or other injury!

When prevention alone is not enough, understanding how physical force is exerted helps us frame appropriate responses and can motivate even the inactive women into defensive training.

The Weapons You Always Carry

Unarmed escapes and defenses should be mandatory training for all girls as they grow up. A girl's or woman's size or stature should be little detriment if the teacher is innovative and the martial art selected is suitable for women's self defense. For example, Aikido techniques work on principles of leverage, so do not depend on weight or size to work against a larger assailant, a factor we can safely predict when discussing women's self defense. Alternatively, I would look beyond fighting styles that emphasize wrestling or grappling, which require upper body strength.

Women need a repertoire of basic defensive skills they can learn in a manageable period of time, perhaps one to two months, with simple, powerful techniques that can be regularly reviewed with friends or partners. These include basic blocks and parries to deflect physical attack, responses to an armed attack and uses of less-than-lethal weapons.

Many students of the martial arts find the physical training and practice relaxing and empowering and will continue training indefinitely. While that is a wonderful experience, it is unfair to deny physical defense skills to students who cannot or will not commit years to the discipline. If among the latter group, consider instructors trained in the Tony Blauer Personal Defense Readiness program[1]. This approach to self defense is simple, easily understood and necessarily brutal. Students get the chance to take on well-padded and protected role-players to go full-force with the techniques they have been taught.

Simply learning new ways to use your body and spirit is the door that motivates some to continue their physical self-defense studies. More than posture, stance is the way you stand to distribute weight and maintain better balance. Breaking habits like standing with knees locked, feet close together or on a line from which balance is easily broken are all part of developing a strong stance that is relaxed yet ready, attuned to Condition Yellow.

Stance and body awareness are the definitive factors in individuals who radiate command presence. This bearing claims and usually receives a respect for personal space. When crowded, either as a "test" or simply by a rude, invasive oaf, strong stance and body awareness makes it natural to simply turn sideways, enlarging your personal space without uttering so much as a word of rebuke.

Another aspect of physical defense training is developing response speed. Attacks happen so quickly there simply is not time to fall back and devise a strategy. If you expect to escape, a harsh, rapidly executed counterattack will be required. Most people wait too long to fight back, whether simply moving off the line of force, discharging pepper spray, or drawing their defensive handgun. Some deny that the attack is truly happening to them, others search in their handbag for the can of pepper spray they dropped in months ago, and still others are caught in what famous instructor John Farnam calls "mental fibrillation," trying to decide what to do. Self-defense training, as well as continued practice and mental rehearsal, are all good preventive medicine for mental fibrillation.

In seeking physical defense instruction, be clear about what you need. Many traditional martial arts have been diluted by tournaments and rules and have lost sight of the defensive necessity from which they evolved. If a self-defense instructor boasts of tournament wins, or shows off elaborate, choreographed sequences and flamboyant high kicks and spins, keep shopping. A street fight doesn't recognize belts or trophies. It is survived by returning simple, vicious physical responses that can be implemented on irregular ground, in darkness or disorientation, and other unfavorable circumstances.

Simple and Vicious

In hand-to-hand defense, the defender must 1) disable the assailant's ability to breathe or see, or 2) impede movement by damaging limbs and extremities. "Disrupt wind, vision, or limbs," advises Phil Messina, founder of Modern Warrior.[2] When you evaluate a defensive art or weapon, ask if it accomplishes at least two of these objectives.

Defense training is often scenario-specific. Women are advised to kick the assailant in the groin or jab him in the eyes. Both strikes are fine if the assailant does not block the groin kick or reflexively deflect the jab to his eyes. Protecting eyes and groin are deeply ingrained human reflexes that can prevent a counterattack from connecting.

In unarmed combat, I'm a strong believer in low kicks to break joints, injure limbs and disrupt balance. Unlike men, women's power is centered in the lower body and legs. A smashing kick to the side of the assailant's knee can break or disable the limb sufficiently for you to escape an attack from side or front. Even a kick and downward shin scrape can momentarily surprise someone making a rear grab enough for you to break free.

Women can deliver a disorienting palm-heel smash to an assailant's face if they are grabbed from the front. Bending the knees and dropping the hips, then rising dynamically to slam all your power up into the palm-heel smash turbocharges the blow.

If you are knocked to the ground, orient your head away from the assailant by spinning on your back. Use your legs to kick and trap the assailant's legs. A strong leg trap can put the assailant on the ground while you roll to your feet to escape or draw a gun. You may not have time to stand or find yourself unable to get up. When deciding where to carry a canister of defense spray or a handgun, be sure you can reach it quickly from a variety of disadvantageous positions and that it won't be lost if a purse or backpack is grabbed.

While every instructor has some favorite empty hand skills, a book isn't the place to learn unarmed defense techniques. You can't learn fighting from a book any better than a written manual can prepare you to pass the road portion of the driver's licensing test. Find martial arts instructors who will work with you on stance and speed, recovery skills to get back on your feet, choke-hold escapes,

A hard palm-heel smash is a disorienting blow that allows the small person to deliver considerable power. Here, Jacqueline practices the steps with a practice partner.

ground-fighting techniques, improvised impact weapons, and weapon retention and disarming. Seek out empty hand techniques you can perform naturally and reflexively to buy the seconds necessary to escape or draw a firearm.

Notes

[1] Tony Blauer Personal Defense Readiness, P. O. Box 278. Victoria Stn., Westmont, PQ, Canada H3Z2V5 www.tonyblauer.com

[2] Modern Warrior, 711 N. Wellwood Ave., Lindenhurst, NY 11757

CHAPTER 11

Non-Lethal Tools

An intermediate (non-lethal) weapon is meant to deflect an assault before it turns lethal, or to gain time and distance to draw and use a gun. The greatest value of non-lethal weaponry may be the legality of open carry. Devices like the Kubotan, mid-sized pepper spray canisters and other tools are legal to carry openly in the hand in many places. Thus their immediate availability is a strong argument for intermediate defensive tools, even if you legally carry a handgun as well.

An intermediate defensive tool is not an appropriate response to a lethal force attack! On the other hand, using a gun or other deadly force is justified only when murder or crippling injury is imminent. Must I wait until I know I'm going to be killed to use some degree of force to stop someone who is hassling me? No! I need to react quickly to employ non-lethal or intermediate force to deflect or escape before the situation becomes deadly.

Finally, in a gun-phobic society, we are finding more and more places where the law prohibits firearms possession. Setting aside the issue of constitutionality, we'll discuss non-lethal weapons to carry from your car into the courtroom, from the parking lot into the post office, through other restricted areas, and in your place of employment.

Pepper Sprays

Pepper spray, an aerosol deterrent that has all but replaced Mace®, has become the most commonly-carried self-defense chemical. Pepper spray is based on oleoresin capsicum (OC), a naturally-occurring chemical compound found in red peppers like chilis and habaneros. OC, compared to earlier chemical restraint agents, can boast greater effectiveness against drug influenced, intoxicated, deranged, and enraged individuals. It is also used as grizzly bear deterrent and is effective against dogs. Only strictly trained attack dogs have been shown to withstand an application of pepper spray.

When pepper spray was gaining popularity between 1987 and 1989, the Federal Bureau of Investigation made extensive studies and tests of pepper sprays. In one report, the FBI showed that virtually 100% of 59 people sprayed suffered some inflammation of mucous

Practice for safety in gun-free zones: Jacqueline drives a mini-baton into the nerve of assailant's leg while tucking her chin as defense against a choking attack.

membranes and upper respiratory systems. Inhaling the spray caused coughing, shortness of breath, gasping and gagging. Eyes closed involuntarily as the OC contacted sensitive tissue. Skin inflammation was common, ranging from redness to acute burning. Perspiring or fair-skinned people suffered greater skin discomfort.

FBI results confirmed a principle also apparent in police reports about OC: success depended on discharging enough OC at the target. The FBI suggested at least one three-second burst or three one-second bursts. Not surprisingly, the FBI tests showed the OC is more effective in enclosed areas, and my experience has shown that the user is very likely to suffer cross-contamination if discharging OC indoors. Be aware that wind will disperse OC if it is sprayed outdoors. Indoors or outside, you need to quickly leave the area after discharging OC into the air, to avoid secondary contamination.

Various reports, combined with personal experience, show that coughing and respiratory discomfort after OC exposure usually diminish in 15 to 20 minutes in fresh, uncontaminated air. Skin irritation may well linger for half an hour or more, burning even after the oily agent is washed away. The best antidote for OC contamination is soap and water to remove it from skin and plenty of running water in which to bathe the eyes. Police often carry Sudecon wipes, but in my experience the wipes do not remove as much of the irritant as does a generous application of soap and water. Generally, the effects of contact with OC spray will disappear in 30 to 45 minutes if the agent is washed away.

Private citizens who discharge OC in self defense should retreat rapidly and then, from a place of safety, call 911 to report the incident and request assistance for the person sprayed.

Pepper spray sounds like a good solution to many self-defense problems. However, it is like any other defensive method: it can fail, especially if the user is untrained or unfamiliar with the delivery system.

The Best Tool For The Job

When and why do aerosol defenses fail? The answers are many and should be thoroughly covered in a user's course taught by a manufacturer-certified or law enforcement-certified trainer. In the private sector, success of an aerosol defense requires that the substance sufficiently distract or hinder an assailant so the intended prey can escape or begin a more forceful defense.

OC spray is marketed in varying intensities, ranging from 2% OC in a base carrier to 17% concentrations. However, the important measurement is stated in Scoville Heat Units, which should be in the 2 million unit range for best results. In selecting an OC spray for intermediate defense, the delivery system is more important than the concentration. Defense spray manufacturers market several delivery systems: an aerosol fog that comes out of the container in a cone-shaped cloud, cans that deliver a thin, solid stream, and foam containing OC.

For civilian self defense, I firmly recommend the cone-shaped aerosol cloud. Your goal is to escape by temporarily distracting the assailant. The stream delivery system affects only the area it contacts, and is harder to deliver to the eyes, nose or mouth, since it is only a

At a pepper spray class at the Firearms Academy of Seattle, Barbara experiments with one of the newer delivery systems, the PepperBlaster, which discharges a pressure-driven stream of OC. The orange practice unit delivers a blue dye, which students were able to evaluate for quantity, dispersal and distance of delivery.

thin stream. The foam carrier may linger on skin, but it has limited effect on respiration and can be blocked from eye contact. The cone-shaped cloud, however, billows out from the container and is difficult to keep out of the nose and lungs and settles on the skin to cause irritation, as well.

Against experienced subjects holding their breath or shielding their eyes, lay down a fog of OC through which they must come to reach you, then move away laterally when they enter the OC. For example, if you are crossing a supermarket parking lot when an assailant rushes at you, yell "Get back! Don't come any closer," in a commanding voice. Have the OC spray ready in your hand. Your non-dominant arm should be fully extended to deflect the assailant and protect the spray canister. If he doesn't obey your command, fog the space between you.

After breathing or contacting the mist, the assailant may crouch defensively and bring his hands to his face and double over protectively. These results are not guaranteed, however. Some people are quite unaffected by pepper spray. Other offenders have experienced it before, so they know they can achieve their goal despite the discomfort. If it does distract the assailant, choose the nearest escape: return to the store or get into your car. Call 911 immediately to report the attempted assault and your use of the chemical defense.

If you discharge the OC you carry, replace the canister after the incident to be sure you have a sufficient quantity if you ever need it again. In all likelihood, your perception of the time lapsed and amount of spray expelled will be distorted by the fight-or-flight experience. When you buy a new canister, give it a brief test spray to be sure the nozzle is functional. You should continue to test the canister every four to six months to be sure the aerosol propellant has not escaped or the nozzle become clogged. Plan to replace OC spray units on a yearly basis. Although the OC remains potent, it is useless inside a defective canister.

If you discharge OC to fend off an assault, you need to move swiftly on an angled path away from the attacker. If you merely back up, the attacker, continuing his forward momentum, can run right into you and finish the assault. Always disengage and run for safety. Don't mistakenly believe that OC is the magic formula that will take an assailant to his knees.

Pepper spray sounds like a wonderful defense tool, doesn't it? I certainly like having it among my defenses. But, please, do not make the mistake of believing it is more effective than it really is.

We possess and learn to use aerosol restraint sprays, empty-hand techniques, and other intermediate weapons to buy the time needed to escape or reach a gun. A spray will not perform well in high wind or at great distances. It takes longer to affect a person wearing a baseball cap and wraparound sunglasses, if it is effective at all. Don't rely entirely on the spray!

Legal Concerns

Despite the common defense tool that it has become, some states restrict purchase, carry and use of OC sprays. Many incorrectly classify the aerosol agent as a "tear gas," which technically is a lachrymator (tear-inducing) agent, while OC is an irritant agent. Restrictions

If you discharge pepper spray, lay down a heavy cloud of the irritant agent between you and the assailant as you escape.

range from age limits for purchase to a licensing requirement. A few states strictly prohibit possessing OC. Violations can result in charges ranging from misdemeanors to felony charges. *Before carrying OC spray, especially if you bought it outside the area in which you wish to carry it, call a local law enforcement agency, the attorney general or municipal attorney and inquire about laws covering its use and possession.*

As of this writing, OC sprays are illegal on commercial airlines, and your canister will be confiscated if detected when you attempt to take it through security with carry-on baggage. More severe penalties are allowed by law. Cabin pressure changes could result in canister leakage, a problem for which you do not want to be responsible. If traveling, it may be better to buy a canister for use during your stay, then give it to your hostess or business associate before flying back home.

Laws and regulations change too frequently to report with any accuracy in this book. Please be responsible for yourself and research the law before obtaining any sort of defensive tool.

"What's That Stick on Your Key Chain?"

The great value of any intermediate weapon is the ability to carry it openly and ready for use, in your hand. During the women's exposition I spoke of at the beginning of this chapter, a few women came up and smugly showed me the small OC canister in their handbag. "That's good," I encouraged, "but you ought to start carrying it in your hand. Don't fool yourself into thinking you can dredge it out of the bottom of your bag when you see trouble."

The most natural intermediate weapon to carry continuously is the mini-baton. It attaches to key rings, and at 5-1/2" long by 5/8" diameter, fits naturally into the hand. Takayuki Kubota developed the first mini-baton in the 1970s for California executives needing a defensive weapon. Looking for items the executives carried regularly, he developed a defense system using the expensive writing pens all the gentlemen used. The pen was later replaced with the grooved metal or plastic mini-baton we know today as the Kubotan.

The Monadnock Company used to produce a similar mini-baton called the "Persuader." Of identical dimensions to the Kubotan, instead of grooves the Persuader has ridges that dig into nerve and bone during certain techniques. The ridged Persuader is less likely to slip off a pressure point than is the grooved version. Nowadays a variety of manufacturers make and sell mini-batons, and these are sold through numerous martial arts suppliers.

Neither the ridged nor the grooved mini-baton is of much value without appropriate training. Mini-baton escape techniques are based on nerve and pressure points. Pressed or jabbed into specific physical locations, the baton causes sharp pain, distracting the assailant. As he loosens his grip or hesitates momentarily, the defender escapes.

Other control techniques employ pain compliance. Applied properly to the wrist, the mini-baton can effectively disengage an assailant who is grabbing the front of your clothing; continued pressure can drive him to the ground. Grabs from behind are countered by driving the end of the baton into the delicate bones on the back of the hand or into selected points on the arm.

Because leverage and pain compliance are at the heart of mini-baton techniques, size disparity is only a limited disadvantage to the petite mini-baton user. However, in teaching Persuader techniques, the Firearms Academy of Seattle staff has run across a few students with very high pain tolerances who exhibit little response to the pain compliance techniques. It is reasonable to expect that as many as one in 15 people can endure this level of pain, so you must be prepared to switch to another tactic if the technique, properly applied, fails to elicit an immediate response. Remain fluid: if the pain compliance approach doesn't work, quickly switch to a destructive technique.

Mini-baton training also includes jabs and flaying with the keys on the end of the baton that can inflict more pain and actual physical injury, depending on the location of the strike. Breaking free of a grab may entail breaking the assailant's fingers by levering them up with the baton. Key flays and destructive techniques are capable of causing great physical injury or even as deadly force, and this type of strike may cost the assailant his vision or result in broken bones or permanent disability. In a fight for your life, however, you are justified in inflicting this kind of harm if no other reasonable alternative exists.

Just as we recognize the uses and shortcomings of pepper spray and other alternative defenses, the mini-baton is not the best defense to every kind of attack. It is extremely valuable, however, for the legality of carrying it in-hand nearly everywhere. The secured areas of airports and aboard airliners are the most common places that prohibit possession of a mini-baton. Most other locations, like post offices, courthouses and schools, allow possession of this small easily carried defensive tool while prohibiting more effective forms of self defense. In these locales, the mini-baton is worth more than its weight in gold.

Facing the Blade

A long impact weapon is superior to the short mini-baton if facing a knife or other contact weapon. Skills with impact weapons such as an expandable baton or aluminum-shafted flashlight offers some help against this terrifying danger. With society skittish about defensive weapons, we are greatly restricted in tools which we can openly carry immediately available in hand. No such restrictions are placed on a 3- or 4-cell flashlight like the Mag-light, however. No one looks twice at a woman crossing a parking lot casually carrying a flashlight, yet one who understands impact weapons and their use can employ this utilitarian instrument quite effectively. The aluminum shaft of a simple C-cell Maglight can become an agile, improvised baton that is capable of injurious strikes, yet no one is worried by its benign presence!

Until you understand just how fast a deadly assault can be acted out, you may be puzzled by all the emphasis on having a defensive tool already in hand. In 1983, research by Dennis Tueller of the Salt Lake City Police Department showed conclusively that an attacker can dash across 21 feet in less than the two seconds it takes a skilled handgunner to draw a pistol and fire two accurate shots (that cannot be expected to take immediate effect). The Tueller study taught us this critical lesson: *maintain an extreme distance from anyone who could pose a cutting or bludgeoning threat; move off the line of force established by a charging attacker; and recognize the absolute and deadly danger of knives and other contact weapons.*

Distance equals survival in a knife fight. Defenses that increase distance between you and the knife-wielding assailant can give you time to draw a gun or escape. A four-cell aluminum flashlight or an expandable baton extends your reach 12 to 20 inches, distancing you

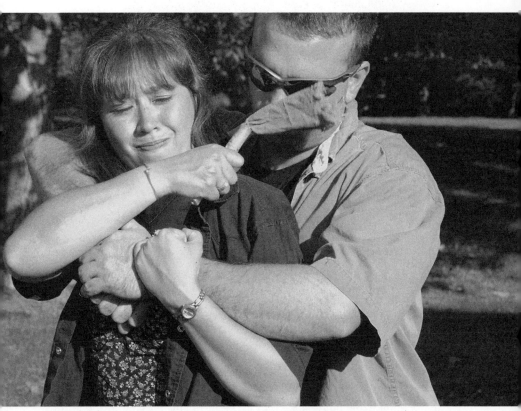

Jacqueline drives the end of her practice mini-baton into the metacarpals of the assailant who has grabbed her. When that technique does not work, she uses a cloth representing the keys usually carried on a mini-baton, to simulate a devastating strike to the assailant's eyes.

from the knife and giving you a striking weapon with which to disable the offender.

Courses in baton use or stick fighting ingrain skills that can put any improvised weapon to effective use. Don't bypass training and go right to the security guard supply store to buy a baton, which may not even be legal for possession by the private citizen in your area. Impact weapons can be grabbed and turned against you viciously if you poke ineffectively at an assailant or even if you make a good strike, then fail to move quickly out of a vulnerable position. Integral to this skill is footwork to keep you in position to inflict injury, while moving out of the way of retaliatory strikes, slashes or kicks.

Some years ago, Calibre Press produced a video titled *Surviving Edged Weapons* that, despite the fact that it is now rather dated, is must-see viewing for anyone at risk from knife-armed assailants. If the scenes depicted on that classic piece of video don't persuade you to seek further training, consider the following: Stabbing survivors frequently report that they were quite unaware of the knife, or other weapon, until they saw their own blood. Any blade can do incredible injury in the hands of even an untrained person, making it a truly fearsome threat.

Contact, puncture and slashing attacks are completed with a variety of utility tools, not just knives. Screwdrivers and other weapons of opportunity are often used with deadly results and can be obtained and possessed by felons with no threat of prosecution. Likewise, boxcutters are legal, available and common tools on many job sites.

While counterintuitive, a rapid and violent defensive reaction is one of the most effective responses to a knife threat or attack with any sort of bludgeon. Called "getting inside," a rapid step inside to control the attacker's arms is an effective first step to subsequently disarming an assailant using a contact weapon. Realistically, moving inside and blocking the arm's arc of motion offers greater control than dodging thrusts and being forced backward, where losing balance is a real hazard.

A forced retreat is extremely dangerous, for the attacker has all the advantages of forward momentum's speed and balance. No one can move back as dynamically as they can press forward, putting the retreating victim at a dangerous disadvantage–one that may cost her life. From the stronger inside position, the trained practitioner can trap the hand or arm to disarm the attacker and counter attack with her own elbow strikes, head butts, eye gouges or leg traps.

Think through what you would and could do if threatened with a knife or with a bludgeon. Keep your defenses simple and immediate. The goal is to disable the assailant, break free and run for safety. If attacked with a knife or other gouging, stabbing or cutting instrument, the odds say injury is extremely likely. *If the crime attempted is simple robbery, by far the wisest course of action is throwing your purse or wallet to the robber and running away if possible.* This is yet another reason to be careful what information is inside your purse or wallet that could lead a thief to your home. Cash should be kept separate from driver's license and proof of automobile insurance or other identifying paperwork, and keys should absolutely be in a pocket or on your person, not in your handbag. These plans deserve attention, and are ideas you can implement immediately to increase your security.

Lies and Dangerous Scams

In a society that does not seem to trust its citizens with deadly force, women are often given dangerously ineffective tools for defense.

"#1 Police Recommended Safety Device!" I read that claim on an ad for a stun gun, and less than a week later was told by a personal alarm sales representative that *their* device was the #1 police-recommended safety device! The truth is that neither is adequate defense in an attack. The stun gun, despite advertisements bragging about 75,000-volt shocks, works only if both terminals are held against the attacker for seven to 10 seconds, until the muscles go into spasm. No one, not even a small person, will compliantly stand still while you press the stun gun's electrified prongs against them. A struggle will break the contact before the muscle spasm can be induced. Why are

Confronted with a contact weapon, Kathy's hands come up so fast that the motion is just a blur! She knows she has almost no time in which to control the attacker's blow.

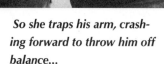

So she traps his arm, crashing forward to throw him off balance...

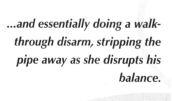

...and essentially doing a walk-through disarm, stripping the pipe away as she disrupts his balance.

women being told to use non-lethal gimmicks against rape and lethal assault?

High-decibel noisemakers are frequently touted as deterrents to assault. The high-pitched siren "will drive him away and bring help," say the promoters. These devices sound much like car alarms. The screech of a car alarm is considered more of a nuisance than a deterrent. If the owner is in hearing range, they can run to the car to quiet the alarm, but no one else, police or otherwise, hurries to investigate the squeal of a car alarm. Do not believe claims that a noisemaker or siren will summon help. It will not.

I do endorse the motion-sensing noisemakers as budget alarm systems, if you can adjust the device so it responds only to gross movement, like the opening of a door or window. Not everyone can afford to pay a major company to install and monitor an alarm system, yet all of us need ways to be sure our doors and windows won't be pried open as we sleep, allowing an intruder in our homes while we are vulnerable. Attach the noisemaker to your sliding patio door or to windows that don't have adequate locks in that primitive cabin you rent for vacation, or the window of the motel room that turns out to be on the ground floor even though you requested second story or higher, and trust it only to alert you if someone breaks in.

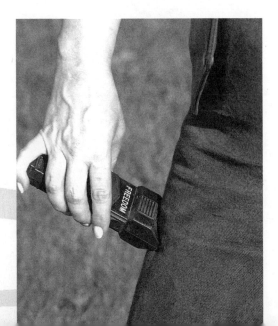

One of the author's favorite demonstrations in women's self-defense classes is holding a stun gun to her leg and pressing the switch. Students are astonished by its ineffectiveness.

Tools Are Only As Good As Your Training

Any self-defense device is only as effective as the training you receive in its use. Even the simple OC spray is most effective when combined with patterns of movement and other good defense tactics. Equally important is the legal defense you muster by presenting training certificates in both non-lethal and firearms defensive techniques. Your training certificates show the prosecutor, judge and jury that you carefully studied appropriate ways to stop varying levels of criminal assault. You can testify that your training was the basis for the method with which you choose to defend self and family.

Legitimate instructors of the mini-baton, oleoresin capsicum/OC spray, stick fighting, or hand-to-hand defenses must inform you that intermediate force is not sufficient against a deadly force attack. Use intermediate defenses to stop harassment before a lethal assault begins, yet always be prepared to answer lethal force with a firearm if that is the kind of attack you face. More about that later.

This high-decibel noisemaker can alert you if someone forces open a vulnerable window, but it is good for nothing more.

CHAPTER 12

Tasers

W ell over a dozen years ago, I sat across the dinner table from John Farnam, one of the most down-to-earth members of the firearms training fraternity, and was openly skeptical when he said he thought that within our lifetimes we would see the technology of self defense advance from firearms to highly effective phase pistols. What seemed fantastic then now seems only one or two new inventions away. Though we aren't quite at the Star Trek stage yet, police and private citizens are fighting back with electrical devices that make the stun guns of a few years ago look like child's toys.

I refer, of course, to the Taser®, a battery-powered electronic control device (ECD) that projects barbed electrical leads into the assailant and applies pulsed electrical current that runs through the neural network. This inhibits voluntary control of skeletal muscles, rendering the subject unable to move, provided that the barbs embed at sufficient distance from one another. Current is transmitted through two barbed probes that are discharged from a one-time use cartridge. When both barbs contact the target, an electrical circuit is created and the electricity acts on the muscles, which contract during the electrical pulse, then relax between pulses, though in reality it happens so quickly that the subject is not aware of the contraction/relaxation cycle.

The Taser C2 model starts its cycle with 17 pulses of electricity measuring about .072 joules per pulse, compared to a cardiac defibrillator, which delivers 150 joules of energy. Pulse frequency is varied during the C2's 30-second cycle, during which the citizen is advised to set down the ECD and run to safety. Nomenclature describing the power delivered by ECDs may sound confusing. When the term "volt" is used in advertisements, it primarily indicates the distance the spark will jump. The Taser uses 50,000 volts, the minimum required to deliver the pulsed current through up to two inches of clothing. This amperage is too low to pose danger of electrocution, but the pulsed delivery infiltrates the human neural network to accomplish incapacitation, according to Dr. Mark Kroll, PhD on Taser's training DVD.

Law enforcement has been using the Taser as an alternative method to control and subdue subjects since the 1990s. In 1999, the Model 18 Advanced Taser was released for civilian use, and in 2002 the model X26C was released to private citizens, though a price tag in excess of $1,000 puts it beyond the budget of most private citizens. In July of 2007, the Taser® C2 Personal Protector came on the market, and with prices of $300-350 depending on options, it looks like the personal Taser is here to stay. Retail outlets like Sports Authority are now stocking the C2 and the unit is sold online as well.

The C2 is a 6"x2"x1.25" ECD with specific operational features that take into account the private citizen's need to stop an attack, but not take the offender into custody. The C2 comes with the manufacturer's offer to replace any unit left behind when it has been used to stop an assailant. All they want is a copy of the police report detailing the incident, something that would probably get to them in any case, due to discharge of miniscule tags bearing the serial number of the Taser cartridge, for law enforcement to collect following Taser use. These, along with the background check required before activation of the C2, are part of the manufacturer's effort to keep their device in responsible hands.

"Was Farnam right?" I wondered after reading all this. Is the C2 Taser a good defense weapon for people who don't want to or can't carry a gun? Or does it fill a defense niche completely separate from the concerns of the armed citizens?

In search of answers, I called a Taser Senior Master Instructor, Chris

The Taser® C2, sometimes called the personal Taser, comes in a variety of amusing colors and patterns.

The Taser® probe cartridge slips into the front of the C2 unit.

A barb at the end of the wire pierces clothing and skin, so when two probes contact an assailant the electricity makes a circuit and flows between the two points of contact.

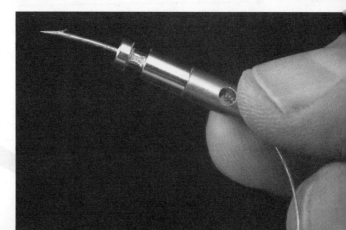

Myers, who is also a partner in the nationally recognized CRT Less Lethal research group in Seattle, Washington. Though very positive about the defense capabilities of the C2, Myers expresses concern that the C2 looks so user-friendly that potential owners won't realize that the tool is of limited value without training and practice. Without training, too many C2s could just take up purse space, where they would not be accessible during a fast-breaking attack.

Myers, a police officer by profession, explains that hesitation to use a weapon against another human being is common, regardless of the self-defense tool employed. Couple that with the difficulty of deciding whether someone walking toward you is just another pedestrian in the parking garage or someone who is about to attack you. Thus we acknowledge the next reality about using the C2 Taser: it will be deployed at very close quarters, as Myers explains.

The citizen's Taser C2 model only has 15-foot probes, compared to the 21- to 35-foot long probes on various police versions. Realistically, a private citizen under attack rarely begins to fight back at any greater distance, simply because many people do not detect the threat at greater distances, or the assailant does not reveal his intentions until he is close enough to grab his victim.

Perhaps this is why the least expensive version of the C2 has no sighting mechanism at all, though the $350 model has a laser sight. Myers is disturbed by the sightless model, explaining, "I cannot imagine using a C2 without the laser sight that is on the more expensive model." When beginners take their first test shots with the C2, the probes commonly go high, because the trigger mechanism is on the top of the unit where it is depressed with the thumb. Under stress, with hand and arm muscles tensing, far too much pressure is imparted to the switch with results similar to a pistol shooter who "milks" the grip by convulsing the entire hand during the trigger pull, Myers suggests.

With Tasers being marketed on the Internet, in retail stores and at the popular new Taser home parties (successor to the Tupperware parties of the 1960s), many C2 units go out with only an informational DVD to educate the new owner. Myers expressed concern that without having ever discharged Taser cartridges (an expensive undertaking at $25 per cartridge), when faced with deploying their Taser, these new owners have little idea what to expect. Without confronting concerns about hurting another human, and having not worked out aiming issues, Myers predicts only limited success. Practice also serves to satisfy the natural human doubt that wonders, "Will it work?" which we face with any defense tool, he concludes.

When asked about classes for private citizens, Steve Tuttle, vice president of communications for Taser, explained that the price of the high-end X26C includes a one-hour training session with a police officer, but for the less expensive C2, the company ships the informational civilian training DVD, though he commented that the possibility of offering training courses with the device in various localities was of interest to the manufacturer.

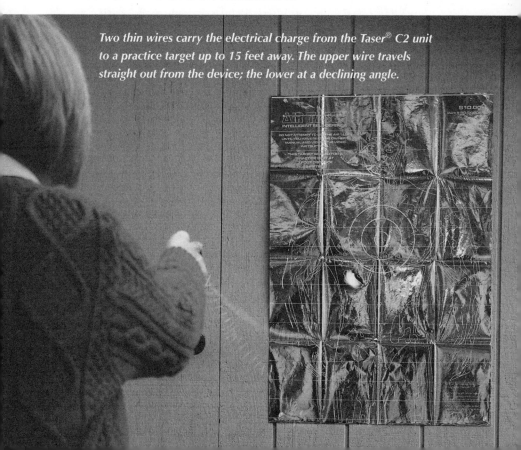

Two thin wires carry the electrical charge from the Taser® C2 unit to a practice target up to 15 feet away. The upper wire travels straight out from the device; the lower at a declining angle.

Myers, on the other hand, repeatedly emphasizes the need to know how the C2 works before relying on it for self defense. "You need to fire the Taser enough until you know where the darts will hit every time," Myers stresses. In this way, self-defense with a C2 Taser is no different from practicing martial arts or learning to shoot a gun.

With proper training and an aggressive determination to defend oneself, Myers believes the C2 Taser is a reasonable defense option. "At this price range, there is simply no competition for the C2 in ECDs," he says. As a veteran patrol officer, he relates that when ECDs were the new tool for police use, law enforcement officers Tased a lot of offenders. Now, when the little red dot of the Taser's aiming laser moves across an offender's chest, he sees a lot more tough guys ready to surrender before things go any further. "The deterrent effect of the Taser laser is huge," Myers exclaims. Women using the C2 could ride on the coat tails of the law enforcement experience and find considerable reluctance from an "experienced" criminal to be Tased, he suggests.

I must emphasize that just like the misconception of "scaring a criminal away by pointing a gun at him," the deterrent effect with a Taser is only as strong as the willingness of the woman holding the Taser to use it! Myers is right: only training and experience give that kind of confidence and determination. Do not get a defense tool without being trained to use it.

Different Applications

Though the recommended use of the Taser entails deploying the probes and embedding the barbs through which the current runs, the C2 model, like law enforcement models, also has the "drive-stun" or contact capacity: you stick the device into the assailant and trigger it. A drive-stun is used if the probes have been discharged but failed to connect, or it might be applied to a second aggressor.

A drive-stun is a pain-compliance technique, and when contact is broken, the pain stops. In my experience, it was easily escaped by simply wrenching away or knocking the device out of contact. Taser

The Taser C2 cartridge.

Even a small circuit created by hooking Taser® probes into Brenden's shirt relatively close together, creates considerable distraction. (Exposure made with subject in kneeling position for safety.)

Brenden experiences a brief exposure to the Taser® C2's power. The circuit created by these close-together probes will not take him to the ground, though it takes his attention off most anything else while the C2 unit is sending electricity down the wires.

recommends pressing the front of the C2 into the assailant's neck if using it for a contact stun. The drive-stun is also useful if only one probe has contacted the offender, because contact can close the circuit. In law enforcement, officers are taught to close the distance to the subject and apply a drive stun to complete the circuit if a probe misses. "This move is a lot more aggressive and requires confidence in the device that it will work," exclaims Myers. Still, this should not be overlooked as a tactic, whether to correct poorly aimed probe deployment or in response to multiple assailants. Reduced to this strategy, however, the woman armed with a C2 cannot follow Taser's advice to leave the C2 on the ground and use the 30-second electrical discharge to run away, so she will need a strategy to escape or overcome the aggressor at some point in the fight.

Author tests a Taser® C2 drive stun as Don simulates a grabbing attack.

Don demonstrates the problem with the drive stun – his ability to break contact and renew his attack.

This is just one more example of the need for education when we add any defensive tool to our resources. Without training, the Taser owner has little idea what to do if only one probe makes it to the assailant. In addition, I concur with Myers that the additional $50 to buy the laser-sighted model is nearly obligatory.

The Taser's role is not limited to non-gun owners. Many gun owners are unable to go to work armed, due to workplace restrictions, and others live in areas where gun ownership is allowed but where licenses to carry a concealed weapon are rarely if ever granted to ordinary people.

Resources

Taser International, 17800 N 85th St., Scottsdale, AZ 85255 800-978-2737 www.taser.com

CHAPTER 13

Rape Prevention and Survival

While we train and take care to prevent sexual violence, it would be utterly foolish for even accomplished martial artists and pistol shooting champions to conclude that we are invulnerable! This chapter incorporates sexual assault information presented in newsletters and brochures made available by the American Women's Self-Defense Association (now Association for Women's Self-Defense Advancement, 556 Ft. 17 N., Ste. 7-209, Paramus, NJ 07652 http://awsda.org 1-800-STOP RAPE)[1] as well as data and details from a variety of women's advocacy organizations, women's counselors, law enforcement sources and more.

Understanding the Crime of Rape

The rapist is driven to control women, either in an expression of power or of anger. Some need to degrade their victim; others are aroused by the terror and anguish their acts cause. For others, the ultimate control of life or death is the key to their crime. In an effort to apprehend rapists, law enforcement psychologists have suggested four different profiles that define most sexual predators. Over 40% are estimated to be "power-assertive" types, typified by the date-rapist who attempts to get a woman vulnerably alone and uses force to gain submission. More spontaneous is the "anger-retaliatory" rapist, who acts out sexual violence to punish and degrade women, subduing his victim through explosive and unexpected violence. Authorities believe this type is responsible for a third of the rapes committed.

One-fifth of rapists are thought to fit the "power-reassurance" model, indicated by low self-confidence and passivity in day-to-day life. Victim selection may start with stalking or peeking in windows. Entering through unsecured windows or doors, exerting minimal physical force, the intruder is likely to make verbal threats regarding a weapon the victim is never shown. This man may act out a fantasy that he is with a lover.

The smallest percentage of rapists fit the description of the "anger-excitation" category. This minority is motivated to inflict pain, and may hold a victim for torture beyond the initial attack. An intelligent and organized criminal, he has rehearsed and planned his crime well in advance, using his charisma to mislead those around him.

The average sentence served by a convicted rapist varies from eight months in the local jail to about eight years in the state prison.[2] Parole, conditional release, or partial supervision puts some rapists back into society much earlier, and many are released from custody before the court's consideration of their initial charges.

We are too often blinded to the presence of these men by our own stereotypes, presuming that we "know" how a rapist looks or acts. Statistics reveal that women are often acquainted with their attacker and have chosen to trust him.

Women cannot assume that they are safe with acquaintances from work, from social or church contacts, or even within their own families. To the contrary, almost two-thirds of all sexual assault victims know their assailant, whether that person is a friend, intimate, or a relative. Too many women have obtained a court order restraining an intimate male offender from further contact, only to find that restraining order useful only in further legal action and of little value in assuring her physical safety. If a spouse, boyfriend or acquaintance harasses or assaults you, your immediate defense is your own responsibility. The police simply cannot arrive in time to stop a determined attacker.

Restraining orders are, however, vital in obtaining cooperation from police and the courts in pressing charges against an abuser. The survivor needs to report the contact to police and keep scrupulously truthful records of restraining order violations, listing dates, times, and descriptions of the incident. Write down your exchange with the abuser and keep a diary of witnesses who can corroborate your account.

Police also use restraining orders as a tool to interrupt the psychological control an abusive mate uses to draw the repeat victim back into his control. More than one abused wife has been freed from ongoing mind-games when the husband violated a no-contact order and landed back in jail for a month or so. Sometimes that is enough time for the woman to establish a new, safer life elsewhere.

Violation of Trust

When women report rape by someone they knew, a quarter of the time an intimate, a husband or boyfriend has committed the assault.[3] Warning signs – even in men who seem very ordinary – include indications that they place little value on what you say or wish. Not listening to your words, interrupting, talking while you are speaking, or ignoring what you say are all signs that should not be disregarded. Doing what he wants despite your explicit request is a huge red flag, even if it is only a choice of restaurants, radio station or other minor issues.

Listen to the jokes, vocabulary and conversations of the men with whom you associate. Notice how they speak of former wives or girl friends. Expressions of hostility toward women, demeaning views about women, or beliefs that women exist to serve men are all harbingers of trouble. Be wary of people who invade your personal space, and when you push them away play mind games to make you feel guilty, prudish or otherwise embarrass you into allowing the invasion. You are being tested for submissiveness.

In dating situations, possessiveness or jealousy is not endearing – it is cause for concern! And finally, heavy drinking or other substance abuse can unpredictably reduce normal barriers to sexually aggressive behavior.

Social activities are important to active, healthy women. In today's world, however, with date rapes frighteningly common, you must exercise caution and common sense at a bar, a party or other gathering. If you go to the rest room or elsewhere, safeguard your drink or do not drink from it when you return. Know where your drink came from. Ask for the unopened bottle or can, watch the bartender mix it or offer at a private gathering to serve yourself. Rohypnol and other sedative/hypnotic drugs are now all too common. Consumed with alcohol, these substances produce disinhibition and amnesia, which is no doubt the reason for their notoriety as "date rape drugs."

An epidemic for women aged 15 to 24, date rape may follow mutually desired contact that exceeds the woman's wishes. Intoxication by either or both parties contributes, but ultimately date rape results from the assailant's contempt for his date's rights and wishes. When this disregard is physically acted out, a crime has been committed.

One of the most difficult aspects of rape by an acquaintance is self-accusation that the violence was the victim's own fault. The survivor suffers the loss of ability to trust others as well as her own judgment. As a result, rape by an acquaintance, especially during a date, is rarely reported and prosecuted. Although physically and psychologically traumatized, some date rape survivors do not identify their trauma as rape, and thus do not seek help from women's counselors skilled in assisting in rape recovery.

Rape is defined as nonconsensual sexual acts completed through violence or threat, or enacted when the victim is physically unable to consent. It is that simple. If the woman says, "No," "stop," or in any other way indicates her unwillingness to participate, or is not consciously able to consent, the sexual activity is nonconsensual. It is that simple. If the aggressor forces intercourse on the woman against her wishes, he commits the crime of rape. Too often responsibility is placed on the victim, who feels unable to stop the sexual activity for fear of immediate physical harm or later reprisal. Blaming the survivor is an ages-old dodge, one you can short-circuit by recognizing and rejecting it.

Rape Prevention

Your determination and mindset, as much as your training, will keep you alive if you are sexually assaulted. Rape prevention training should include physical defense methods, weapons skills and panic control. Your training will help you keep a level head, because it has prepared you to choose the right response without any wasted thought. Expect to feel the fear, yet remember that you have been trained and know how to protect yourself. Use your mind to interrupt the panic.

Don't expect to dissuade the rapist by pleading, stalling, reasoning or crying. Remember that a predator rapes as a means to control and degrade his victim. *Establish your unwillingness to be his victim.* Take the first opportunity to resist and escape when you find a window of opportunity. Use your own body or any object available – a bedside lamp, the corner of a hard-bound book, a bottle picked up from the street – to smash an attacker's face, nose, eyes, Adam's apple, knee or groin.

Look for a way to fight back and escape immediately instead of "hoping" for a chance later. Any vigorously-enacted defensive plan promises more success than thinking of the perfect plan after it is too late. Many women escape abduction by running and screaming before the predator has them fully under control. Statistics show that a combination of forceful verbal commands and physical resistance provides the greatest chance of stopping a sexual assault. Be prepared to back up verbal resistance with physical violence whether or not you possess a gun.

Rape is a deadly force attack. Sometimes the rapist uses verbal threats and the intimidation of his greater physical size and strength to force the victim's compliance. Although a knife may not be at your throat, nonconsensual intercourse is still an attack on your life because the rapist implies that he will use any degree of force necessary to overcome your resistance. Too often men trivialize the severity of rape by arguing that no one was ever killed by a penis or mockingly suggest that victims should "lie back and enjoy it." This cruel stupidity discourages women from fighting back and often convinces society there is little reason to prosecute rapists, and it clearly communicates that society does not acknowledge the violence a rapist inflicts against his victim. Deadly force is completely justified against a rapist because it is his threats of death or crippling injury that cause the victim to submit to nonconsensual intercourse.

Understand, also, that you are capable of resisting a rapist, whether armed or not. Knives are frequently used in rape attacks, and prior training can help you survive against a knife as discussed in the previous chapter. Remember, you may be cut and may bleed, but use this knowledge to avoid panic and keep fighting to gain your freedom. With proper training, you can disarm a knife-armed or gun-carrying assailant. As often as not, an audacious, unexpectedly violent counterattack so surprises the assailant that his plan is derailed when the survivor is not terrified into submission.

Early, dynamic resistance can short-circuit life-threatening danger during and after the rape. *Don't allow yourself to be tied up or otherwise restrained or put into a vehicle. The majority of victims who are restrained are murdered during the assault.* It is better to fight for your life while you can actively resist, than to trust your survival to the predator later.

For decades, women have been warned not to resist rape, counseled by men and police officials who understood neither the effects of rape on the victim, nor the rapist's motivation. Refuse to believe anyone who does not value your life and survival enough to allow you to use forceful defensive tactics and effective weapons to preserve your life.

One leading argument against putting up a fight was the imagined danger to the intended victim. Citing National Crime Victim Survey data, researcher Don Kates reports, "The gun-armed resister was actually much less likely to be injured than the non-resister who was, in turn, much less likely to be injured than those who resisted without a gun. Only 12 to 17% of gun-armed resisters were injured. Those who submitted to the felons' demands were twice as likely to be injured (gratuitously [after the rape or incident]). Those resisting without guns were three times as likely to be injured as those (resisting) with guns."[4]

No one can teach you specific sets of movements to stop a rapist since each attack is unique. Instead, learn elemental principles of physical defense, and if attacked, fight back immediately and assertively. Inflict the most damage you can with the tools you have, even if that is only your empty hands.

Women in an unarmed skills class practice breaking away from grabbing attack then responding with dummy guns. Though the subject is serious to them, their enjoyment shows on their faces.

If You Are Raped

Avoid panic during the attack. *Never give up.* If the rapist prevails, remain alert to escape possibilities that may open up during the assault. Never conclude that you are defeated. With increasing frequency, rapists kill their victims to avoid identification and arrest or for their own satisfaction. Do not consider the attack over until the rapist is truly gone. When he is gone, get to a safe place or if the attack has taken place in your home, secure the house when he has departed. Along with summoning law enforcement and medical aid, call a trusted friend or family member who can come to support and watch over you.

If attacked by a stranger, memorize details about his height and weight, if only by comparing height to a door frame or sign post. Notice clothing he wears and look for distinctive physical characteristics like a muscular or thin physique, his complexion tone, scars, tattoos or blemishes, hair and eye color. If he drives a car, try to determine make, model, color and license number and state, or at least some of these details. If you can't determine the make of the car, try to remember the emblem on the car well enough to sketch it for an investigator. If attacked outside your home, leave your fingerprints everywhere you possibly can, drop personal items that can be identified as yours, including buttons, jewelry, gloves or cosmetic cases bearing your fingerprints.

Disagreeable as it sounds, sexual assault investigators hope that rape survivors will avoid bathing, and changing or washing clothing after an attack, to preserve the maximum evidence for prosecution of the crime. Avoid cleaning your nails or applying medication, they request. For example, we are taught that in cases of oral rape, evidence has been destroyed by as simple an act as drinking water or brushing teeth. Your body holds important evidence that is needed to prosecute the attacker.

A thorough investigation of the crime and the place it happened must be conducted. The investigators need to discuss the assault in detail and may ask questions that seem offensive or senseless, yet are important in preparation to arrest and prosecute the rapist.

A friend can accompany you during the investigation and go with you to a hospital for examination and treatment. You may want to take along a change of clothing as what you were wearing during the assault may be held as important evidence. If you prefer to interact with a female police officer, ask the investigators if one is available or request a women's advocate who is familiar with the post-assault process and can guide you through it gently. An advocate is unencumbered by the emotional response a family member or close friend may feel, and she knows how the system works. In short, an advocate is a valuable member of your recovery team and you should not hesitate to ask the police to call this professional. Many cities have rape crisis centers that provide women's advocates and can later recommend a counselor and help you find legal advice.

Don't be talked out of pressing criminal charges by anyone, including the rapist, your family or others with influence over you. Rapists frequently threaten retribution if you report the assault, and family members, employers or land lords may pressure you for silence if they fear embarrassment or social or financial loss. Your testimony, often joining with the testimony of other victims, can reduce the chance that the rapist will commit the same crime against someone else.

Recovery: Stages of Trauma, Denial and Resolution

The first could be characterized by fear: fear of being alone, which may continue for some time, and is usually especially acute directly after the attack; fear of retaliation; fear of men, all men. Fear meshes with emotions of anger, feelings of helplessness, guilt, pain, degradation or anxiety. Physical manifestations are classic Post Traumatic Stress Disorder (PTSD) problems, and these join conditions directly linked to the rape, like sexually transmitted diseases and physical injury.

Denial can consume a long time, during which some survivors work maniacally to regain control of their lives and well-being. It is an uphill climb, if the trauma of the rape has not yet been confronted. Sometimes, unresolved issues manifest themselves in poor concentration, inability to respond in an emergency, trouble maintaining relationships, irritability, sleep and eating disorders, and other symptoms that indicate post-traumatic stress disorder (PTSD).

PTSD sufferers endure vivid and disturbing memories: reliving the violence in flashbacks or nightmares, emotional numbness and isolation, hyper-vigilance and excessively sensitive startle responses, feelings of betrayal and anger, trouble building trust, as well as physiological symptoms like backaches, headaches, chronic pain syndrome, appetite disturbance and subsequently poor nutrition. The rape can taint healthy sexual enjoyment for periods lasting from six months to years after the assault. Alcohol or drug addiction afflicts

A trusted confidant can give understanding and the strength to go on for one going through the difficult time of recovery.

many PTSD victims, but temporarily-numbed memories or emotions can rebound with a vengeance when such crutches are removed. Depression, ranging from occasional to continual, can also last for quite a long time. Not surprisingly, those who are able to talk to a counselor or trusted friends suffer depression less severely and in shorter duration.

In recovery, the survivor comes to understand that although she is responsible for her own actions, she must never be held responsible or blamed for the actions of another person – especially those of the rapist. *The attack is not her fault, and regardless of the circumstances around and preceding the attack, the rapist's actions remain absolutely inexcusable.*

Recovery takes time and requires a safe environment and a nonjudgmental atmosphere that allows the survivor to work through the anxieties, emotions and physical symptoms. It is a complicated problem, one that should not be faced without professional help and the love of friends and family.

Notes

[1] Association for Women's Self-Defense Advancement, 556 Ft. 17 N., Ste. 7-209, Paramus, NJ 07652 http://awsda.org 1-888-STOP RAPE.

[2] Carney, Kathryn M, "Rape: The paradigmatic hate crime." St. John's Law Review. Spring 2001.

[3] "Prevalence, Incidence, and Consequences of Violence Against Women," Findings from the National Violence Against Women Survey, Nov. 2000.

[4] Kates, Don B., *Guns, Murder and the Constitution*, 1991.

CHAPTER 14

When Am I Allowed to Shoot?

U p to this point, we have discussed various means of self defense, lethal and non-lethal. In the following chapters we'll focus on the safe, responsible use of firearms as self-defense tools.

I don't think very many first-time gun owners immediately realize the power and resultant responsibility they assume when they take possession of a gun. I know longtime gun owners who talk as though they haven't a clue about their responsibilities if a situation prompts them to draw a gun. I'm as uneasy with people who loudly proclaim, "If anyone tries to break into my house, I'll shoot 'em right through the door," as I am with someone who has a gun but is convinced she could never shoot another human, even to stop a lethal assault.

When does the law allow me to use my gun in self defense? The question deals with issues of legality, morality and just plain common sense. The first issue, legality, varies from state to state, and is subject to the mood of the prosecutors and judges currently serving in your area. In our current age of internet computer access, there is little excuse for ignorance of the laws governing possession and defensive use of firearms. An afternoon of browsing through laws and statutes about use of force, self defense, and gun possession posted on most if not all states' websites is a necessary responsibility for the armed citizen.

There are some broad parameters that define justifiable use of lethal force, however, and I credit Massad Ayoob's excellent instruction and writings for the information that follows. Meeting Ayoob, listening to his lectures, and later assisting in teaching his classes have strengthened both my determination and my caution in matters of self defense. As we discuss the principles of justifiable use of lethal force, I think you'll discern the constant interplay of caution and courage.

The legal and the moral codes underlying self defense have some foundation in plain old common sense. Our standard should be, "What would be the response of a reasonable and prudent person, under the same circumstances and knowing what you knew at the time?" This is the concept of reasonableness as introduced by Ayoob in his lectures on judicious use of deadly force.[1] Most instructors who

Deadly danger consists of the ability of an attacker, the opportunity to use force against the victim, and the personal jeopardy so obviously posed by the attack.

address lethal force teach that the presence of three elements is required to justify using lethal force: ability, opportunity and jeopardy. Let's analyze each element.

Ability: If using lethal force in self defense, the survivor must be able to show that the attacker had the ability to kill or cripple. Presence of a deadly weapon, greater numbers, or superior physical size and strength all demonstrate ability.

Opportunity: Did the assailant have the opportunity to harm you? You cannot shoot a person who threatens to choke you from across a crowded street because he could not possibly enact the threat without laying his hands on you. Opportunity exists only when the threat can be acted out with such immediacy that the intended victim cannot escape.

Jeopardy: Has the assailant put your life in jeopardy? Verbal threats and gestures alone do not justify using deadly force unless the assailant's actions make it clear he intends to kill or cripple you immediately.

In Your Own Home

Do different rules apply inside the confines of your own home?

Suppose you hear noises in the basement during the daytime. Home alone, you take your loaded gun to investigate. This is no time to burst in, gun drawn with your finger on the trigger. You must know the intruder's identity before firing a panicked shot into a landlord, repair worker or other person authorized to be there.

I had owned my first gun less than a year when early one evening my landlady entered my apartment unannounced. She thought I wasn't at home, but that didn't lessen my surprise. Fortunately, I had received training that prompted me to issue a verbal challenge before pointing the gun at the opening door. Did I have a gun in my hand? You bet. Did the landlady know that? No, nor did she need to know. As has proven true in so many situations, training provided the confidence to act with discretion and to take the time to fully assess the situation, even in the grip of fear.

Unlike your duty to retreat if assailed on the street, there are few if any jurisdictions that require you to leave your own home to escape an intruder. Evan Marshall, a well-recognized author in firearms and law-enforcement publications now retired after 20 years with Detroit's police force, told me that during all his years as a homicide detective, he never saw a citizen prosecuted for shooting a criminal who had forced entry into an occupied home.

The individual's right to defend the sanctity of the home is upheld by most state laws and municipal codes. In civil court, however, the

Certain this stranger has no just reason to enter the home, the citizen facing this terrifying specter is allowed considerable latitude in her defensive response.

intruder or his survivors may charge that you overreacted or behaved recklessly, depriving them of the benefit of their son, husband or father's support. Despite the widespread legal latitude about shooting home intruders, this is just one of the reasons we assiduously avoid shooting whenever possible.

The decision to shoot must be based only on an inescapable threat to yourself or other innocent occupants of the home, never on panic. If you or occupants of your home participate in illegal activities that could result in a police raid, you must consider how to deal with law enforcement officers entering to serve an arrest or search warrant.

Armed citizens should accept responsibility to live by higher standards than the average American. Part of this responsibility includes adopting a lifestyle that avoids entanglements such as illegal drug use, theft and other crimes. If sharing a dwelling with roommates, you will to some degree share the peril of illegal activities in which they may engage. Choose your companions carefully. In any case, gun store commandos and internet chat groups exaggerate the frequency of "no knock" and surprise police raids. While officers use surprise to successfully serve search and arrest warrants, unannounced entry is scarcely a common or accepted tactic.

Finally, you must not shoot a criminal as he flees from your home. You may not shoot him as he is escaping. Some argue that you may kill a burglar as he escapes with your television or computer, but that seems quite uncivilized to me and is expressly unlawful in numerous jurisdictions. Let him leave; the cost of that television is tiny compared to the legal fees you could incur defending yourself from a civil lawsuit for crippling or killing this person.

Notes

[1]See Ayoob's lecture on DVD, *Judicious Use of Deadly Force*, sold by Police Bookshelf, op cit.

CHAPTER 15

Safe Gun Habits to Live By

W e have spoken in previous chapters about various means of self defense. We have referred, in passing, to the defensive role that firearms can play in well-trained hands. In the following pages, we will specifically discuss the safe and responsible use of firearms as women's self-defense tools.

"They said the gun was unloaded." Have you ever heard these words?

Uncounted firearms tragedies are "explained" by people who believed the gun they held was not loaded. You can prevent enormous tragedy if you always treat every gun as if it is loaded...even if you just unloaded and put it down or if someone tells you, "It's OK, it's not loaded."

The Four Rules of Gun Safety

The sages of the firearms fraternity have correctly noted that gun safety is a state of mind. Although we enjoy firearms of all types in a variety of shooting sports and recreation, a gun must never be considered capable of anything less than lethal results. Strict adherence to a few sensible safety rules will prevent the vast majority of negligent or unintentional firearms discharges. These are taught in many of the world's leading firearms training schools as the Four Universal Gun Safety Rules and begin with TREAT ALL GUNS AS IF THEY ARE ALWAYS LOADED.

Do not accept that a semi-automatic pistol is unloaded until you have carefully checked it by both sight and feel, assuring that the chamber is empty and that the magazine well contains no magazine.

At the gun store or shooting range, check any gun you are handed to determine that it is indeed unloaded. Before too much involvement with firearms, complete a basic gun safety class, so you have the skills to safely check or unload common firearms.

Learn to check for ammunition in the gun by both sight and feel. Some semi-automatic pistols have chambers that are obscured by the slide even when the action is locked open. It is likewise easy to miss a cartridge in the chamber of a bolt action rifle if checking visually. A round of ammunition may be in the chamber, ready to fire if the trigger is pulled. By probing with a finger, you can detect the presence of a cartridge you cannot see. Training yourself to verify an empty gun by sight and feel increases understanding of the gun you intend to use under the stress of a self-defense emergency, sometimes in darkness or other unfavorable conditions.

Next, safe gun handling demands that you NEVER POINT THE GUN AT ANYTHING YOU ARE NOT WILLING TO SHOOT. This second rule applies equally to loaded and unloaded guns. Always know at what and

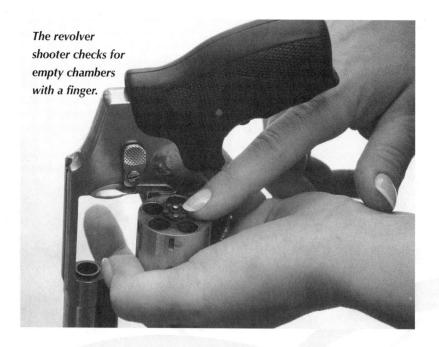

The revolver shooter checks for empty chambers with a finger.

whom the gun muzzle will point. Determine a safe muzzle direction before picking up the weapon – that way you won't cross yourself or someone else with the muzzle while you look for a safe place to point it. And remember, a visual obstruction, like a sheet rock wall, will not stop bullets. Avoid handling firearms off the range unless you are safely practicing dry fire, cleaning the gun, or securing it for the night. Don't show off the gun like a toy or curiosity. Off the range, treat your personal protection weapon as a very private item, even more personal than lingerie or cosmetics.

Treat every gun as if it is loaded; and never point a gun at anything you are not willing to shoot. These are the first rules of safe gun handling. The third rule, KEEP YOUR FINGER OUTSIDE THE TRIGGER GUARD UNTIL YOUR SIGHTS ARE ON TARGET AND YOU HAVE DECIDED TO SHOOT is equally important.

Suppose you hear noises in the kitchen some night. Gun in hand, you go downstairs to investigate. As you approach, the noises continue. You are convinced you will soon face an unknown intruder. In the grip of this stress and fear, unexpected noise or movement will alarm you. If startled, your muscles will contract as part of the body's natural fight-or-flight response. When the fingers gripping the handgun convulse, the trigger finger also contracts. It can do nothing else: in this reflexive state the hand's fingers respond as one unit.

If the finger rests on the trigger, the trigger will be pulled. On a single-action semi-auto, this pretty much guarantees that an unintentional shot will be fired. A revolver or double-action semi-auto is only slightly less likely to be fired during the startle response.

In more ordinary day-to-day circumstances, keeping the finger off the trigger will prevent almost all the negligent gun discharges. High quality guns of modern design don't just discharge by themselves. Someone has to press the trigger. Never break the safety rules because you think the gun is unloaded. Your actions are the basis for habits that will be repeated under circumstances that are not safe.

Learning to keep the finger off the trigger until the sights are on target and the decision to shoot is made. This requires careful attention until the habit is well formed.

Range Time

Spend the $150 to join a local rifle and pistol club, or pay $20 to rent a lane at an indoor gun range where a safety officer is present all the time. Shooting in isolated areas is a dangerous activity, not only because of thieves, also because of unsupervised, hazardous gun handling by "weekend warriors" sharing the shooting area.

Informal outdoor shooting areas also pose great peril to hikers, dirt bikers or careless children who may come over your backstop. When you fire your gun, you must know that your target is safe to shoot at, as well as being certain what is behind that target. The fourth universal gun safety rule is KNOW THAT YOUR TARGET IS SAFE TO SHOOT AND THAT IT IS SAFE TO SHOOT INTO THE AREA BEYOND. I believe this safety rule is probably the strongest argument against shooting in the woods or at a gravel pit. You must know the terminal resting place of each bullet you fire. On a formal range, bullet traps or earthen berms provide backstops to catch the bullet.

Handgun cartridges expel bullets that can travel from 1 to 1-1/2 miles; unimpeded rifle rounds can come to rest from 1-1/2 to 2-3/4 miles from the point at which they were fired. Do not discharge a gun if you do not know where the bullet will land. You must know that the area between your muzzle and the bullet's terminal resting spot is empty of people or property that could be harmed.

Even if you shoot at an indoor range, take responsibility to keep the area safe while you are there. Don't be afraid to correct unsafe gun handling by others or notify the range safety officer of safety violations. If you complain that guns have been pointed at you and the offense continues uncorrected, leave the range because it is not safe. People become over-stimulated while shooting, and just because they claim the weapon is unloaded is no guarantee that they haven't removed the magazine, but forgotten to eject the round from the chamber. Do not accept this or any other explanation as a valid reason to violate the safe muzzle direction rule.

Make Sure Ammunition and Gun are the Same Caliber

Be careful that the ammunition you buy and shoot is the correct caliber for your firearm. Some ammunition-gun misfits are more readily apparent than others. For example, the powerful .357 Magnum cartridge is identical in diameter to the .38 Special cartridge, but it cannot be fired in a .38 Special caliber handgun because it is slightly longer, preventing the .38's cylinder from closing. In other instances, smaller cartridges will fit in the chamber of a larger caliber gun, and dangers include malfunctions that happen when the case doesn't eject from a semi auto, as well as bursting the cartridge's case wall as it expands when the powder is burning.

You can be certain you've bought the correct ammunition, if the caliber shown on the box corresponds exactly with the caliber stamped into the frame or barrel of your firearm. If you're not sure you have the right caliber of ammunition, ask a knowledgeable gun store clerk for advice.

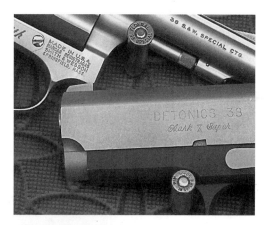

The difference between .38 Special and .38 Super has confused many a beginner over the years.

The .38 Special shown at the left is a revolver cartridge, while the .38 Super is for a semi-auto. Differences in overall length as well as the rim are obvious on closer inspection.

The handgun's caliber is marked on the barrel. Be sure it matches the caliber of ammunition, as identified on the case head of most cartridges, as well as in greater detail on the ammunition box. If uncertain, do not shoot.

If you own several handguns of different calibers, only fire one at a time when you're at the range. For example, set out the .380 ACP and its ammunition. When you're done firing the little gun, put it away and bring out the 9mm semi-auto. While the .380 ACP ammunition may fire in the 9mm barrel, the case rarely extracts properly. We'll have more to say about handgun ammunition later.

Protect Your Senses

On a firing range you must protect your hearing and vision, both of which may be damaged by gunfire. Repeated exposure to gunshots has robbed a lot of shooters of their hearing. At a minimum, use foam protectors inserted deeply into the ear canal to block the noise when you go to the range. Good quality ear muffs are the better choice, since they block more of the noise. Muffs also cover the sound-conducting bones around the ear that transmit damagingly loud concussions. Many beginning shooters display an exaggerated flinching reaction when shooting their handgun. There are several reasons for the flinch that we'll discuss later, but one is the anticipation of the painfully loud noise. That's avoidable with a $20 to $30 investment in hearing protection ear muffs.

Equally important is tightly fitting, wraparound eye protection. When shooting a semi-automatic, or shooting beside someone with a semi-automatic, you quickly realize that the bullet isn't the only object expelled from the gun. The semi-auto ejects the empty metallic case from the fired cartridge. The hot metal case burns when it falls between the lens of safety glasses and lodges on the shooter's cheek. Be sure your safety glasses fit tightly at the eye brow and extend to your temples.

Flying brass cartridge cases are a common problem. Less common, yet posing a much greater threat of injury, is the possibility that an ammunition cartridge may be defective and blow apart the revolver or semi-automatic pistol. If this happens, debris flies in every direction. In other instances, a semi-auto itself malfunctions, and an unlocked breach at the moment the cartridge is detonated allows parts of the brass case to break out and fly in all directions like a little grenade. Both are sobering accidents and can blind unprotected eyes.

Buy safety glasses designed as protection against industrial accidents. The polycarbonate material needs to meet or exceed the ANSI Z 87.1 Industrial Standards for impact resistance. Do not trust your drugstore sunglasses or fashionable prescription spectacles to do the job!

Finally, just owning safety gear is not enough. The ear muffs and protective safety glasses must be put on before entering the shooting range and remain in place until leaving the range. Although you may not be actively shooting, the noise and bullets of others who are shooting can damage your eyes and ears.

No, I'm not suggesting you'll be shot when I say, "bullets." Any experienced shooter has felt the problem of "bounce-backs." While good ranges are designed and maintained to prevent part or all of the expended bullet from ricocheting or bouncing back toward shooters, inevitably some do. A tiny shred of metal bullet jacket lodged in a cheek or chin is uncomfortable, but usually can be removed with a pair of tweezers. If it strikes an eye, instead, the injury is agonizing and removal requires a trip to the doctor. Other times, the entire bullet strikes a stone in the backstop, part of a metallic target holder or other object and bounces back. While its return velocity is considerably slower, a bounce-back can break skin and will certainly bruise.

Lost vision and hearing are irreplaceable. Protect both carefully while on the firing range.

Invisible Hazards

A less apparent shooting hazard is the lead particulate matter generated when ammunition is discharged. Shooters need to protect themselves against lead contamination and take steps to avoid being poisoned.

With a few limited exceptions, firing a cartridge of ammunition releases lead into the air in two ways. If the projectile is a bare lead bullet or had exposed lead portions, lead shavings are created when the bullet is discharged. Even if the bullet is fully encased in copper, nylon or another covering, lead is expelled during the firing process, because most primers contain lead styphnate. When it is detonated, a cloud of molecular lead compounds is released. Lead is airborne when firearms are discharged, and settles on horizontal surfaces like the floor, shooting benches, window sills, and even the hair, clothing and skin of shooters present on the range.

If you pick up empty cartridge cases from the floor – either in pursuit of range cleanliness or to reload the cases – take special care with hygiene. Put the brass into a sealable plastic bag, and wash carefully when the job is done. During range time, make a conscious effort to keep hands and objects away from the mouth, and when you leave the firing line, wash your hands and around your mouth without delay. Do it immediately, before you unconsciously touch your face or eat, drink or smoke. At the same time, take a tissue and vigorously blow your nose to discharge the dust and particles captured by the small nose hairs.

Like many shooting professionals, 99% of the ammunition I shoot is loaded with full metal jacket (FMJ) bullets. This eliminates much of the lead particulate in air and on surfaces. I think avid shooters who are on the range more than once a week are crazy if they continue to shoot unjacketed lead bullets. Lead-free primers are also marketed, though they are far less common than fully jacketed bullets, cost more and are reputed to be subject to degradation from humidity as well as somewhat prone to misfires. In short, so-called nontoxic primed ammunition is a small percentage of what most people shoot.

Women of child bearing age owe it to themselves to be particularly careful about lead contamination, as lead can be stored in the bones to later be mobilized by a variety of physical conditions including pregnancy and lactation.[1] Research by the Reproductive Toxicology Center of Columbia Hospital for Women Medical Center cites studies that give a severe warning about lead exposure in pregnant women. "Lead can be readily transferred across the placenta to the fetus."[2] Stillbirth and miscarriages are common problems associated with lead poisoning.

Risks to Pregnancy

The question of firing range safety for pregnant women and their unborn children is one fraught with highly emotional opinions. I am certain that in response to this section a number of women will report that they shot regularly while pregnant and little Johnnie or darling Susie has come into the world quite unharmed. From a less anecdotal viewpoint, however, I believe there is compelling reason to avoid live gunfire during pregnancy. Lead toxicity and the potential for birth defects is alone very compelling reason to stay away from live fire during pregnancy and breast-feeding.

Some have hypothesized that the potential for hearing loss is further reason to give up shooting during pregnancy. Liquid is an astounding medium for sound transmission with sound waves traveling four times faster in water than in air. Thus the amniotic fluid in which the fetus rests cannot be expected to muffle gunshots or other loud noises, and may magnify sound instead. On the other hand, medical studies reported in Vol. 78 of *Obstetrics & Gynecology* suggest that the liquid environment and the fluid filling the fetus' developing hearing organs may reduce "the risk of mechanical trauma." We have, of course, no means of measuring what actually happens.

For the expectant mother, the wide selection of air guns marketed allows continued marksmanship and defensive firearms practice. Plinking practice with these quieter, cleaner tools keeps the draw and fire motions quick and smooth, as well as maintaining the skills of quick sight picture acquisition and smooth, surprise trigger break, all skills that transfer quite well to the conventional firearm the expectant mother may be carrying for the defense of herself and her unborn child.

Other Dangers

When learning and practicing gun safety, we acknowledge that handling guns can be a dangerous activity. Without a clear understanding of the mechanical function of your firearm, there are additional risks. For example, when a revolver is discharged, some of the gases created by the burning powder escape from the gap between the front face of the cylinder and the forcing cone and can burn close-by skin. While burns from the gas and punctures from lead shaved off the bullet as it goes through the forcing cone are minor compared to a gunshot wound, the revolver shooter should be aware of the hazard. The hands belong on the grip panels. If practicing one-handed shooting, the unoccupied hand should be held far away from the gun, preferably anchored somewhere on the body.

Handling just ammunition alone is relatively safe. The cartridge's function is to expel the bullet from the mouth of the cartridge case into a gun barrel, where the gas pressures are harnessed behind the bullet. If struck squarely and with sufficient strength, a primer can spark and ignite gunpowder outside the gun. Without the chamber walls to contain the pressures created by the burning powder, the bullet doesn't go anywhere, so the hazard is not from gunshot wounds. Instead, extreme pressures rupture the sides of the metallic cartridge case in a tiny grenade effect. Now, it requires intentional effort to dent something so small as a centerfire cartridge primer, although curious children have sometimes managed to do so. Ammunition, as well as guns, should be kept away from unsupervised youngsters until they are responsible enough to be trusted and to understand the hazards.

During unloading, instead of allowing the hand to grasp far forward on the slide, grip the slide at the rear serration. Gripped thus, if the worst possible happens, the hand is well out of the blast zone.

Safe Habits Offset Dangers

Guns can be dangerous! You'll get no argument from me, but we must also recognize that a number of other useful inventions, including automobiles, chain saws, matches, even knives or scissors are dangerous, too.

Much has been written and broadcast about "dangerous guns." Our society has literally become phobic about the small mechanical device known as the firearm. If fear and emotion could be set aside, we would be forced to acknowledge that a firearm is an inert assemblage of mechanical parts designed to perform one function. Without emotion, we would recognize that function as accurately discharging bullets for a variety of purposes, ranging from warfare to hunting, competitive shooting to self defense. Similarly, a larger mechanical device, the automobile, serves a useful function, yet is grossly subject to misuses that cost thousands of lives. Amazingly, society does not loathe cars! We could say the same about power tools.

Practically every aspect of our physical existence is fraught with danger. We harness tools and other elements to offset some of these

Hot gas and bullet shavings escape at the gap between the forcing cone and the cylinder face of the revolver. Keep hands well away!

Safe semi-automatic pistol manipulation requires the shooter to grasp the slide well behind the ejection port.

hazards. In so doing, we tacitly agree to adhere to rules of general safety, as elemental as containing fire in the fireplace so it doesn't burn the house down when we heat with wood. The gun has its own safety rules. If you choose to own any firearm, it is your responsibility to learn, practice and make these safety tenets a habit.

Always Remember!

TREAT ALL GUNS AS IF THEY ARE ALWAYS LOADED.

NEVER POINT THE GUN AT ANYTHING YOU ARE NOT
  WILLING TO SHOOT.

KEEP YOUR FINGER OUTSIDE THE TRIGGER GUARD UNTIL
  YOUR SIGHTS ARE ON TARGET AND YOU HAVE DECIDED
  TO SHOOT.

KNOW THAT YOUR TARGET IS SAFE TO SHOOT AND THAT IT
  IS SAFE TO SHOOT INTO THE AREA BEYOND.

Notes

1 "Lead in bone: Implications for toxicology during pregnancy and lactation," Silbergeld E., *Environ Health Perspect* 91: 63-70, 1991.

2 "Transfer of lead to the human feotus from Moneral Metabolism in Pediatrics," Barltrop D and Burland WL, eds., Blackwell Scientific Publ., Oxford, 1969, pp 135-151.

CHAPTER 16

Basic Firearms Training

Trigger control and sight alignment are both are both part of the pure skill of shooting accurately. Beyond these skills are additional concerns specific to self-defense shooting. The self-defense shooter must guarantee consistently accurate shots on demand, avoiding misses that endanger innocent bystanders – a very demanding standard indeed.

The question of how much marksmanship training is enough varies from individual to individual. I believe anyone who carries a handgun for defense needs to study and practice tactical drills that require making split-second decisions, as well as practicing accurate shot placement. These skills far exceed being able to place five shots at your leisure in the X ring of a paper target!

A male friend or lover may not be the best choice to teach you to shoot. Some men can become decent marksmen without adopting a technically correct shooting stance, because the mass and strength in a man's upper body better overpowers the recoil. The female physique typically has much less upper body mass and musculature to absorb the handgun's recoil. Conversely, a woman's legs are her stronger limbs and she can position her body to take advantage of this strength. Women's smaller, thinner hands grip the gun and manipulate the trigger differently.

The intimidating task of learning to defend oneself with a deadly weapon is a job better approached without the emotional baggage of a male-female relationship. At this point, you need a respected teacher, not a beloved friend. Self-defense issues that have nothing to do with shooting ability also need to be addressed. Women will have different concerns, and, to some degree, different limits governing their use of deadly force. A classroom format that allows you to learn with other women or with women as well as men should encourage discussion of female-specific issues in self defense and in shooting.

Take time to find a training course that is sensitive to women's concerns about self defense. Check the phone directory for a list of firearms or handgun instructors, or start by visiting the gun shops and commercial shooting ranges in your area. Ask for names of people in the area who offer beginning defensive handgun instruction.

After compiling a list of likely candidates, contact these instructors and ask for a résumé of their credentials. Ask about their philosophy of women's self defense, with whom they trained, the length of their experience as an instructor, if they participate in competitive shooting events, and explore their attitude toward women. Get to know the

Some women prefer the women's-only class option, making it easier to ask questions and get help with shooting problems.

mindset of your potential instructor. Ask if they discuss local firearms laws and use of deadly force, along with live fire instruction. Ask for a brief written course description for their beginning shooting classes. An excellent starting place is a handgun safety seminar or an introduction to handguns. An inexpensive one-day or evening course gives you a chance to decide if you like the instructor's teaching style and the opportunity to learn about other training offered. That, however, is only the beginning.

What to Look for

A basic defensive firearms course should include an awful lot more than learning to shoot accurately. Is the world's best target-shooter prepared to save her own life if she is not truly convinced of her right to use the firearm to stop a violent assault? When I teach beginners, I answer many questions about appropriate use of deadly force. If you can't find an instructor who includes material on the use of deadly force in their curriculum, obtain and read Massad Ayoob's book *In the Gravest Extreme* as recommended earlier. At the very least, educate yourself about your responsibility as an armed citizen by logging on to your state's law website by computer, or visit the law library at your

Ruger's Model 22/45 is a perfect gun for the beginning semi-auto shooter, as it works much like larger caliber semi-autos, but its inexpensive .22 LR ammunition has minimal recoil.

county courthouse to read up on your area's firearms and self-defense law. Finally, the National Rifle Association's basic firearms classes include instruction by local law enforcement, attorneys or prosecutors to expose gun owners to this vital legal information. Call their headquarters for the number of an instructor near you.[1]

Next, I believe a basic handgun course should provide beginning students with appropriate training guns and ammunition, allowing hands-on experience before they even buy a gun. First-time shooters learn the fundamentals of marksmanship most easily with the low-recoil .22 LR caliber revolver and semi-automatic. After becoming safe and proficient with a training gun, the student can move on to a caliber that is big enough for self defense. Many beginners can avoid buying a gun that's not right for them by joining a friendly, low-key class with the handguns and ammunition supplied. They learn to shoot, have the chance to ask many questions about handguns and defensive ammunition, concealed carry, safety, maintenance and cleaning of the weapons, all before dealing with the expense and intricacies of their first gun purchase.

Professional training is a responsibility you should fulfill before getting a gun for self defense. If you absolutely cannot find competent training in your area, arrangements can be made for qualified instructors to come to your area or you can travel to one of the nationally recognized defensive shooting schools footnoted below.[2]

When beginning training is complete and elementary questions answered, the student is able to present herself knowledgeably at a gun counter and fend off the patronizing suggestions that the little lady needs a pretty little gun – maybe this .25 caliber with the fake pearl grips. The educated woman can respond with the brand and model number of a 9mm or .38 Special she has already tried out at class.

Next, buying a gun and ammunition for self defense.

Notes

[1] National Rifle Association, 703-267-1000.

[2] Lethal Force Institute, P. O. Box 122, Concord, NH 03301, 800-624-9049; John and Vicki Farnam's Defense Training International, P. O. Box 917, Laporte, CO 80535, 970-482-2520; Thunder Ranch, 96747 Hwy 140 E., Lakeview, OR 97630, 541-947-4104. Additional training resources can be found at the website of the Armed Citizens Legal Defense Network at http://www.armedcitizensnetwork.com/Instructors.html

CHAPTER 17

Annie, Get Your Gun

Years ago, when I asked Massad Ayoob what guns he recommends to women, he said my question was a lot like asking a carpenter if you should buy a hammer or a saw for a building project: "What do you need to do with the tool?" he asked. A gun for home defense can be considerably larger than a gun for concealed carry. A person who can afford just one gun may have to consider its concealability beneath clothes for both hot and cold weather. Someone who can afford a summer gun and a winter gun, or a carry gun and a competition gun, must look for guns on which controls such as the manual safety and magazine release are in similar locations.

I asked the same question of retired cop and fellow gunwriter Charles Petty, and thought he summed it up best when he said, "The best handgun is the one you have with you when you need it." He went on to add that, due to the importance of shot placement, an individual's best self-defense handgun choice is one with which they can hit accurately every time they shoot.

Training classes and shooting experiences lead to the right choice of which Petty speaks. After beginning classes have given you the knowledge to handle guns safely, seek out a public shooting range that rents handguns. Here you can try out a variety of operating systems with varied features and in differing calibers.

Handguns are categorized into two basic types: revolvers and semi-automatic pistols. To help make sense of the great variety of handguns available, let's spend some time learning about different gun types and how they work.

Revolvers

The double-action revolver is the simpler of the two. Take a look at the diagram so the terms are more meaningful. Modern double-action revolvers fire when the trigger is pulled, simultaneously compressing the mainspring and cocking (drawing back) the hammer. At the same time, the trigger pull moves the cylinder to line up a chamber (and, if it is loaded, a cartridge of ammunition) with the firing pin. At the end of the trigger pull the hammer is released and falls, making the firing pin strike the primer and firing the cartridge.

On some revolvers the firing pin is integral with the hammer and strikes the cartridge as described above. On other brands of revolvers, the hammer is flat-tipped and strikes a transfer bar, which carries the

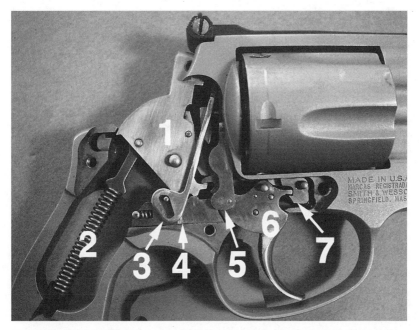

Internals of the Smith & Wesson double action revolver include 1) hammer; 2) mainspring; 3) hammer block, which keeps hammer from hitting cartridge in case hammer stud breaks; 4) rebound slide, which moves trigger back into position once it is released; 5) hand, which moves cylinder into next position; 6) trigger; and 7) cylinder stop, which holds the cylinder in alignment with the barrel.

This revolver uses the design in which the firing pin is integral to the hammer.

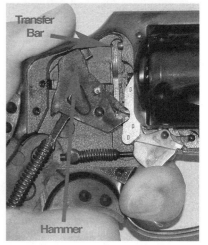

The transfer bar of a Taurus revolver is rising into the position from which it transfers the hammer blow to the firing pin.

impact to a spring-loaded firing pin. The blow overcomes the firing pin spring and the firing pin jolts forward to hit the cartridge primer. In either case, when the primer is hit, the impact sparks the primer compound, and the spark ignites the gunpowder.

An older-fashioned revolver design is the single-action revolver, in which the shooter must manually cock the hammer before firing each shot. Manually cocking the hammer before each shot renders this action type too slow for self-defense work, but it is a fun type of gun for plinking and for sports like Cowboy Action Shooting.

Handguns must be cocked to fire and how this occurs is reflected in nomenclature like single-action, double-action or double-action-only. A cocked hammer is one that has been drawn back so there is some distance between it and the firing pin. Drawing back the hammer lines up two internal parts, the hammer hook and the shelf of the sear. When they engage, the hammer will remain under spring pressure in the cocked position until light pressure on the trigger releases the sear from the hook and lets the hammer slam forward.

On the double-action revolver, cocking can be accomplished in two ways: the shooter can manually pull the hammer back (thumb cocking), or continuous pressure on the trigger will both cock and fire the revolver (trigger cocking). When the trigger is pressed through the final 1/16" or so of the trigger pull, the hammer is released and slams forward. Many self defense revolvers have concealed hammers and thus operate in double-action-only (DAO) mode. DAO revolvers include the Smith & Wesson Centennial lines, as well as revolvers with

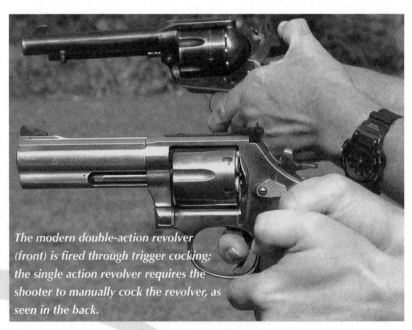

The modern double-action revolver (front) is fired through trigger cocking; the single action revolver requires the shooter to manually cock the revolver, as seen in the back.

The hammer of this Smith & Wesson Model 640 is shrouded, so it will not snag on concealment clothing. It is a double-action-only revolver.

bobbed hammers, including Taurus' CIA model and the older M85CH, and Ruger's SP101 bobbed hammer variation.

Semi-automatics

The semi-automatic (or semi-auto) handgun cocks the hammer in one of two ways: slide-cocking or trigger cocking. When firing the first shot, or when we manually cycle the autoloader's slide (colloquially called "racking the slide") we manually cock the hammer (unless the gun design has an automatic de-cocking mechanism).

When the semi-automatic fires, the expanding gas generated by the burning gunpowder pushes the bullet out of the cartridge case and down the barrel, as is the process with any other modern firearm. As the bullet leaves the semi-automatic's barrel, the gas pressure also propels the slide rearward, so it cocks the hammer again. The extractor, a small hook set in the slide at the ejection port, catches the rim of the now-empty cartridge case and jerks it out of the chamber. After traveling briefly rearward, the empty case strikes the ejector and is flipped out of the ejection port.

When the slide reaches the end of its rearward travel, it is pushed forward by the recoil spring, which was compressed when the slide recoiled. As the slide slams forward, it lifts a fresh round of ammunition from the magazine and pushes it into the chamber. When the round is in the chamber, the slide locks with the barrel (called "in battery") and is ready to fire another round if the trigger is pulled again.

Like revolvers, semi-automatics can be either single-action or double-action. In a single-action semi-automatic, the hammer is cocked manually (unless we have just chambered a round by racking the slide, which automatically cocks the hammer). In a double-action semi-automatic, a long squeeze of the trigger cocks and releases the hammer.

Pressures from the firing ammunition send the semi-auto slide to the rear, ejecting the empty case and re-cocking the action of this Taurus Millenium pistol.

Disassembled Glock slide set up to show the role of the semi-auto's extractor, the small "hook" seen to the lower left, holding on to the case rim.

Confused? Relax. You won't be after your first range session with a qualified, firearms instructor.

After firing, most semi-automatics return to a cocked state. The safety of single-action semi-automatics should be engaged when the shooter brings the sights off target. A double-action semi-automatic should be decocked by mechanically lowering the hammer and placing the trigger in the far-forward double-action position. Many double-action semi-automatics have no manual safety; in these, the long trigger pull acts as its own safety. This carry mode for the double-action semi-automatic is no different from that of the double action revolver, considered one of the safest handguns made. Some double action semi-automatics also have a manual safety that can be engaged, blocking the trigger or hammer (gun designs differ) for further safety.

The traditional double-action semi-automatic initially cocks the hammer the same way as the revolver, with a long pull of the trigger compressing the mainspring. Trigger pressure compresses the mainspring and draws the hammer back into a cocked position, then the end of the pull disconnects the sear from the hammer and allows it to fall forward onto the firing pin. After the first shot, the slide's cycle (discussed earlier) automatically re-cocks the hammer, so subsequent trigger pulls much are shorter and lighter.

To manually cock a double-action gun, the hammer is held beneath the shooter's thumb and pressed down until it catches in the single action notch. As the thumb pulls the hammer back, the trigger moves to the rear, leaving only a short trigger pull, often about 1/8", from which the gun will fire with very little pressure on the trigger.

Decockers

Many modern semi-automatic pistols feature a decocking lever that lets the owner safely lower the cocked hammer from single-action to double-action mode. The semi-auto is slide-cocked and the trigger returns to single-action after the slide has cycled, either from manually chambering a round or after firing. A double-action trigger pull that

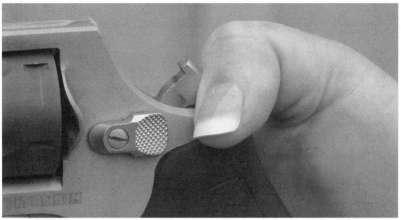

Manually cocking a double-action gun.

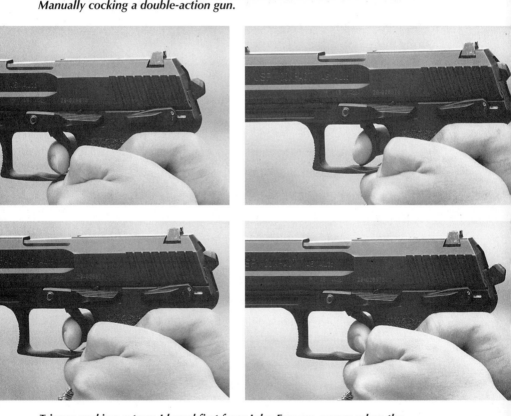

Trigger cocking, a term I heard first from John Farnam, occurs when the shooter presses the trigger of a traditional double action semi-auto, causing the hammer to draw back to a cocked position, as is occurring on this HK USP. This is also how we generally shoot the double-action revolver as well.

requires a concerted effort to fire the gun (12 to 15 lbs. of pressure) is safer, so the hammer should be decocked whenever the gun is no longer aimed into the target.

Years ago, during my first months of teaching women's handgun classes, a new gun owner reported on the first morning of class that her new gun was defective because when she depressed what she believed was the safety lever "the gun would fire!" With consternation, my assistant and I listened carefully as she explained why she was certain this was the case. Experimenting with the unloaded gun the night before class, our student found that when she pressed down on the lever that served as both manual safety and decocking lever, the hammer fell forward, just as she had observed during live fire with other handguns.

When sold her new semi-automatic pistol, she was not introduced to the decocking feature, so she naturally feared if it lowered the hammer it would also discharge the gun. Her pistol was functioning exactly as it was designed to, but she hadn't realized that. A wonderful feature of women-only gun classes is the ability to clear up such mechanical misunderstandings – and other topics – without embarrassment or further confusion!

Examples of semi-automatics that can be manually decocked include older Rugers, third-generation Smith & Wessons, the Walther PPK, SIG Sauer's P239 and similar models, and Beretta and Taurus semi-autos and some variants in Heckler & Koch's USP line. Some, like HK USPs, can be carried either decocked only, decocked and put on-safe, or placed on-safe in single action.

Still other semi-auto pistols can fire from and customarily are placed in double-action mode, but lack a decocking mechanism. These are not impossible to put into double-action, though the operation requires a safe, bulletproof backstop since the procedure involves working the trigger and carefully lowering the hammer by hand.

After the slide cycles, this Smith & Wesson Model 3913 is both cocked and off-safe.

The shooter thumbs down the decocking lever, and the Smith & Wesson's decocking mechanism safely lowers the hammer without discharging the gun.

Single-action Semi-autos

Other semi-automatic pistols have single-action-only (SAO) triggers with no other option available. Single-action semi-automatics must be cocked to fire, too, and the trigger cannot accomplish that task. The single-action semi-automatic is cocked when the slide is "racked." Every shot through the single action semi-auto fires with the same light pressure and short trigger pull. Probably the most famous single-action-only semi-auto is the .45-caliber 1911-style pistol, which you will frequently encounter on the firing range.

The excellent SIG P239 has a decocking lever conveniently positioned on the side of the frame, here beneath the shooter's thumb.

After the shooter depresses the decocking lever, the SIG P239's hammer is safely lowered and the gun can be holstered.

The single-action trigger pull is short and generally requires only three to six lbs. pressure to discharge the gun. The hammer must be cocked for the gun to fire, either by racking the slide to chamber the round or by the slide's rearward movement during the firing cycle. When loaded and cocked but not being fired, these guns' safeties must

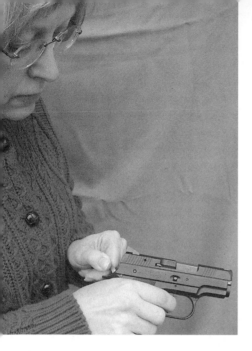

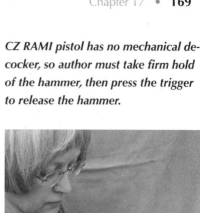

CZ RAMI pistol has no mechanical de-cocker, so author must take firm hold of the hammer, then press the trigger to release the hammer.

She slowly and gently lets the hammer down until it rests in the de-cocked position. Now, if she wishes to fire the gun, a long, heavy trigger pull will precede the first shot.

Whew! The hammer is safely down and the CZ RAMI is in double-action, where it will be most safely carried.

be engaged, often by flicking a frame-mounted lever up. Examples of single action handguns include the Colt, Springfield, Para-Ordnance and Kimber Government Model 1911-style guns and their clones, as well as Browning Hi Powers and handguns by less prominent manufacturers.

The industry added to traditional gun terminology when it coined

The single-action semi-auto, illustrated here by a Springfield Armory 1911, is cocked when the shooter racks the slide to load a round into the chamber.

When firing cycles the slide, ejecting the empty case as seen here, it will again cock the hammer.

the expression "double-action-only." While double action is used to describe a gun fired through trigger cocking, a Double Action Only (DAO) firearm is one that has no provision for manual cocking – for example, a revolver with a bobbed or shrouded hammer or a semi-auto pistol that mechanically and automatically lowers the hammer, decocking the gun, after each shot.

Double-action-only semi-autos are designed to return the trigger to the long, far-forward position after each shot and are represented by Beretta's Model 92D and by Ruger's P89 DAO, to name only a few. The term "double-action-only" is in my opinion inaccurately applied to semi-automatic pistols that are striker-fired, such as the Glock line, Kahr handguns and others. These pistols have no hammer, so the striker is held under spring pressure until movement of the trigger moves a plunger that blocks the striker, freeing it to go forward and hit the primer.

Stopping Power: How Big Is Big Enough?

Before discussing defensive caliber and gun choices, it must be reiterated that no firearm or ammunition is guaranteed to stop an assailant. Individuals have differing capacities to withstand gunshot wounds. Self defense may require a number of shots to stop an assailant, especially if he is enraged, insane or using drugs. Acknowledging that there is no magic gun or bullet, let's discuss the best choices available.

When considering a handgun for self defense, a minimum caliber should be the .38 Special revolver loaded with at least +P ammunition, unless you have compelling reasons for choosing a smaller caliber. (See Ammunition, Chapter 18). Many believe the .380 ACP ammunition is powerful enough to stop an assailant, and indeed, stories are told in which the round performed admirably. Yet, a confrontation with an assailant is dangerous enough without the disadvantage of a gun selected for small size and light recoil, but lacking the power to quickly stop a deadly assault.

Ruger entered the striker-fired semi-auto market in the fall of 2007 with the 9mm SR9.

Glocks, Kahr Arms, Smith & Wesson's M&P pistol, and Ruger's SR9 pistol have no hammers, but use a spring-loaded striker that is released through the trigger pull to hit the primer.

At one time, people chose the .380 ACP, because it was the only handgun small enough for easy concealment. Today, several manufacturers sell 9mm handguns that are literally as small as most .380s. Before compromising on a .380 ACP pistol, at least try the 9mm Kahr Mk9 handgun or the 9mm Smith & Wesson CS9. The .380 ACP cartridge has a small, light bullet that needs to be loaded to higher velocities to increase the likelihood it will stop an assailant, and even then it is not very powerful.

Guns that chamber ammunition smaller than .380 ACP are not sufficiently powerful for reliable use in self defense. Historically, .22 LR or .25 ACP caliber guns have failed to decisively stop assaults. The bullet doesn't transfer enough energy to do much damage in body tissue. Probably the best hope for someone armed with a .25 caliber handgun is to try to penetrate to the brain's medulla oblongata, yet these kinds of shots are very difficult, if not impossible, in dynamic self-defense situations. .22 LR ammunition may possibly be more effective than the .25, but the little bullets have a troubling tendency to zip through tissue, making only a small wound channel and causing only slow bleeding unless striking the spinal cord or brain's medulla.

People have certainly perished from small-caliber wounds, although death usually occurs later from blood loss or much later from untreated infection. In self defense, the intent is to use a weapon of sufficient caliber to stop an assault decisively before you are injured. As a self-defense shooter, your goal is not the death of the assailant, rather to put an immediate stop to the assault.

The .380 ACP semi-automatic may be considered by people who suffer reduced hand strength, and who will practice and train to become extremely accurate with their gun. After one of our training courses, a student who suffers from degenerative arthritis chose a mid-sized Beretta Model 86 .380 caliber semi-automatic. This gun's barrel tips up so the shooter can chamber the first round without having to manually cycle the slide, making it an excellent choice for people with physical conditions that diminish strength. These folks must continue to practice and take classes, to ensure undoubtedly that they can deliver rapid, accurate fire in self defense.

In other useful roles, the .380 ACP semi-automatic is often carried as a back-up gun worn on the ankle or in a pocket holster as a second gun, insurance against malfunction or failure by a primary gun of larger caliber.

Another important consideration in gun selection is the amount of time you are willing to commit to training and maintenance. *If you have little time to train, you will be better served by the revolver.* If you are interested in shooting and can budget time for good training, frequent practice, and regular maintenance you can benefit from the semi-automatic's ease of shooting and ergonomic design.

Effective handgun selection requires truthful answers to several more questions. Does the buyer have sufficient upper body strength to work the slide of a semi-automatic gun? If you do not have much hand strength, you may find the slide of many semi-autos very difficult to manipulate. Remember, you have to manually cycle the slide for a lot more than just unloading the gun. The slide has to be drawn back to chamber the first round, to clear malfunctions, and to disassemble and clean the weapon after shooting practice. If it sounds like too much work, consider the user-friendly revolver.

I Like It, but Does it Fit?

The buyer next needs to assure the proper fit of the gun in her hand. The index finger's last joint must contact the center of the trigger when the grip tang is centered in the hand's web. It's nearly impossible to shoot a double action gun accurately with only the tip of the finger touching the trigger.

Don't be fooled by gun salesclerks who say, "Slide your hand down on the grips," or "just move your hand around until your finger reaches the trigger." The web of your hand must be on the backstrap of the gun so the trigger finger can make a natural, straight-back pull for accurate shooting. A bad fit that lets the grip tang ride against the thumb's base knuckle will transfer the recoil into the bony joint with every shot fired,

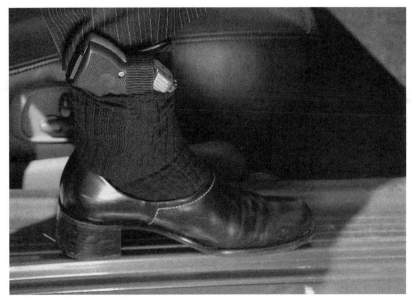

A .380 North American Arms Guardian worn in an ankle holster requires more frequent cleaning than a revolver carried in the same place, due to the demands of its mechanical function. Still, most women can conceal the thin little semi-auto, where a small revolver would bulge on the ankle.

resulting in poor recoil control, shooting discomfort, and eventual joint injury.

After assuring that the gun's backstrap-to-trigger dimension fits your hand, you may find that certain design features make some guns easier, or harder, to shoot than others. The relationship of the bore (barrel) to the shooter's wrist can make a gun easy to fire accurately – or it can add hours of training to overcome the gun's upward recoil.

Handgun designs that closely align the barrel with the wrist and arm transfer the recoil directly into the shooter's palm and web of the hand, fleshy areas that can absorb the impact painlessly. Because the low barrel aligns with skeletal support of the wrist and arm, the muzzle rises less during shooting. With increased recoil control, the shooter can quickly get the sights back on target for rapid consecutive shots, an important consideration in self defense against multiple assailants or a single assailant who is not stopped by the first few shots.

Sometimes women struggle to lock open the semi-auto's action. One tried-and-proven technique is punching the gun forward with a dynamic twist of the hips while the non-dominant hand pulls the slide to the rear.

A related technique to maximize strength for semi-auto slide manipulation is locking the dominant side arm tight against the rib cage, then racking the slide.

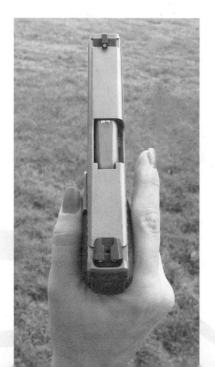

If attempting to lock the action open, it is critical that the thumb be in position beneath the slide stop lever ready to push up when you have the slide pulled all the way to the rear. This is a simultaneous motion that new shooters sometimes fail to understand. Many shooters twist their hand slightly around the gun to get the thumb into position to push up on the lever.

In addition, the low bore axis takes advantage of the human ability to raise the arm and accurately point the index finger at the center of an object. When a gun fits the hand perfectly, the sights are nearly lined up when you point the gun at the target, due to the good ergonomic relationship of the gun to the hand and arm.

Examples of low-bore-axis semi-automatics include pistols from Kahr Arms, Glock and the Heckler & Koch P7M8. The Smith and Wesson Centennial revolver has an unusually high backstrap that results in a low bore axis for an extremely pointable .357 Magnum or .38 Special caliber revolver.

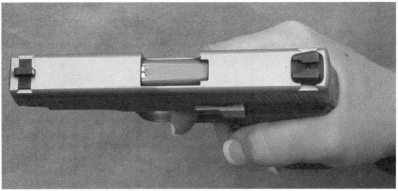

Proper handgun fit: with the gun's backstrap centered on the web of the hand, the crease of the trigger finger's first joint contacts the trigger face.

This large Glock Model 29 is a wonderful handgun, but not for someone with this size of hand.

If I Can Only Have One, Which Should I Choose?

Most first-time gun owners buy their weapon thinking it will be the only handgun they'll ever own. Later, many shooters find they need to refine their selection after experience introduces them to better fitting or functioning guns; others graduate from a gun bought for in-house defense to a smaller gun that they can carry with them everywhere. If, at the outset, the buyer is looking for an all-around gun, a moderately compact handgun is the best choice.

A number of .38 Special revolvers fit that description. Good choices include the premium Smith & Wesson Centennial line, which features a completely shrouded hammer, or the bobbed hammer Taurus Model 85CH or their CIA line of affordable revolvers. Both are good revolver choices for concealment beneath clothing that could catch on the hammer when drawing the gun.

Small five-shot revolvers fit small hands well and are comfortable to conceal. Holstered inside the waistband, the revolver's round cylinder can be uncomfortable without a well-made holster. Six-shot revolvers, allowing room for that extra cartridge, have larger cylinders that may poke the wearer's tummy or hip.

Revolvers with exposed hammers can be entrusted to a gunsmith to bob the hammer, with results similar to the Taurus M85CH. I would consider the Ruger SP101 for such an operation. Because the .357 Magnum is chambered in the same SP101 frame as the .38 Special, I would buy this heavy-hitting .357, then practice primarily with lighter .38 Special ammunition. Since the .357 Magnum case is only slightly longer than the .38 Special's, a .357 Magnum revolver can fire .38 Special ammunition for reduced recoil or for economical practice. The same is applicable to the lighter, more slightly built Smith & Wesson revolvers, but the lighter the gun, the more recoil is felt when shooting. This becomes truly unpleasant with the lightest-weight alloy-framed revolvers.

New or Used? Stock or Custom?

When money is really, really tight, budget revolvers are generally a safer choice than cheap semi-automatics because of the simpler design of the revolver. In 2008, off-brand .38 Special revolvers were marketed for around $350 – considerably less than the $700 price on the smoother and more widely recognized Smith & Wesson brand, $570 for a Ruger, or $400 for a good Taurus Model 605. Used revolvers should be even more affordable. Novice buyers should not overlook the savings of buying a used revolver. Have a gunsmith look it over, checking for damage, like a bulged barrel or excessive play in a locked cylinder, and cracks and wear on the frame and topstrap. There's simply less to go wrong on a used revolver than on a secondhand semi-automatic, which is trickier to buy used.

Revolver selection requires the buyer to think about concealability, frame size, fit in the hand, and possibly about after-market replacement grips, too. A revolver's backstrap-to-trigger dimension can be adjusted by replacing the factory-installed grips with after-market grips or different grips may be chosen to increase or decrease the circumference of the grips and to fill in the void between the back of the trigger guard and the frontstrap. Large rubbery grips provide more material to absorb the recoil and make it easier to maintain a strong hold under recoil.

Chris Cunningham custom crafted this woman's holster to go with the custom gunsmithing her husband Grant did on the S&W Model 60 5-shot revolver it carries.

Combination of .357 Magnum ammunition in snubby revolver creates more recoil than will prove practical for many. Although the author is exaggerating for the camera a little bit, this combination is truly unpleasant to shoot, and most will do better choosing a gun and caliber that produce less recoil.

Control of the muzzle rise during recoil improves here due to strong stance and grip, but more than a dozen shots is sure to cause sore, aching hands!

Semi-automatic features give the buyer nearly endless choices in magazine capacity, trigger action, frame size and location of safeties, slide locks and magazine releases, but fewer choices of how the gun fits in your hand, because replacement grips are less common than for revolvers. Many semi-automatic grips are integral to the frame and cannot be changed, so the original fit of the weapon is crucial. The polymer-framed Glock pistol is an example of a gun that needs to fit right the first time, since the grip is composed of the same molded polymer as the frame. Of course, for several hundred dollars that grip can be reduced by one of several gunsmiths specializing in this after-market alteration.

You may find certain semi-automatic pistols easier to shoot effectively than others. Several compact semi-autos that are easy to carry, conceal and shoot include the 9mm Kahr Arms line of pistols, Glock subcompacts, Smith & Wesson's 3913 or 3953, a 9mm with 8-round capacity magazines; Heckler & Koch's P7M8, a unique 9mm with 8+1 round capacity; and single action semi-autos of the 1911 variety, now made by several manufacturers in smaller calibers than the original .45 ACP.

Women often appreciate the short trigger reach of the high-capacity Glock handguns, and those with really small hands are very enthusiastic about the small pistols in Kahr Arms' product line. Caliber choices include 9mm, .40 S&W and .45 ACP calibers.

Glocks, like many guns introduced in the 1980s and 1990s, use a "double-stack" high-capacity magazine. Instead of positioning the bullets one atop another, as in a single-stack, low capacity magazine, the bullets are staggered zigzag. A double-stack magazine results in a slightly wider grip that may compromise the gun's fit in your hand and make it a little harder to conceal under clothing. The Kahr pistol, using a single stack magazine, is much smaller in grip size and ammunition capacity. Both are striker-fired and have no thumb safety.

Compared to high-capacity semi-autos, a 1911 Officer's model, the HK P7M8 and S&W 3913 or Chief's Special 9mm are extremely flat and easy to carry. For concealed carry by a trained individual, the advantage of high capacity handguns over their smaller, more easily concealed six- or 8-round counterparts is all but obliterated. I don't believe high capacity is as important as concealability in handgun choice for the armed citizen, for whom accuracy with several initial rounds is far more important than 12 to 17 cartridges in one magazine. Remember, how well the gun fits your hand is translated directly into shooting accuracy.

Right between the 9mm and the big-bore .45 ACP caliber is the .40 S&W caliber. Developed by Smith & Wesson, this caliber of ammunition is correctly referred to as .40 S&W, to give credit to

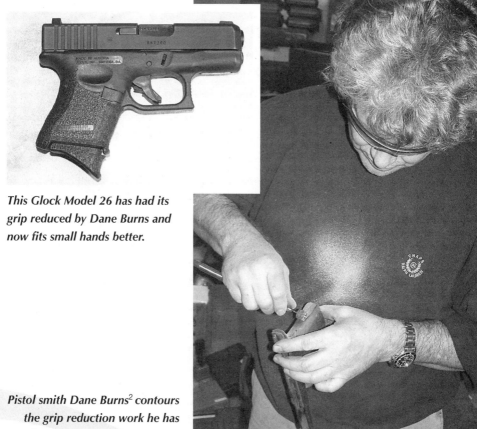

This Glock Model 26 has had its grip reduced by Dane Burns and now fits small hands better.

Pistol smith Dane Burns[2] contours the grip reduction work he has performed on a Glock Model 27.

the developer, although all the major manufacturers sell handguns in this caliber. Ballistically, the .40 has shown stopping power that is better than the 9mm, and it is estimated that +P .40 ammunition should approach the optimum results of the .357 Magnum based on documented shootings by police. Examples of .40 caliber handguns include the Glock Models 22 and 23, Smith & Wesson Models 4013 and 411, Heckler & Koch USP, Kahr K40, Ruger P91, several models of SIG-Sauer pistols and others including the EAA Witness.

When our students shoot guns provided for live-fire demonstration, they are excited to discover they can manage the .45 ACPs recoil. With the development of high performance .45 hollowpoint ammunition, the venerable .45 has become an even better self-defense handgun. Reacting to the call for lighter, faster bullets, several major manufacturers load a 185-grain .45 caliber bullet that leaves the barrel at around 1150 feet per second.

Good choices for concealable .45s include SIG Arms' P245, Kimber's Ultra Carry, Colt's Lightweight Commander, Officer's Model or the even smaller Defender, subcompacts from Para Ordnance and Springfield's Ultra Compact .45. A full-sized .45 with a 4 1/2 inch or 5 inch barrel will be a better choice for competitive shooting, training or to serve solely as a home-defense gun since the compact .45s recoil viciously.

An individual's ability to shoot well with a particular handgun and caliber is influenced by upper body strength plus hand size and strength as well as the caliber and dimensions of the gun. Buying a gun recommended by a large number of men may yield a man-sized gun, but one you can't shoot effectively. A fit of machismo when buying a gun is dangerous!

While the gun's fit in your hand can be determined in the sterile atmosphere of a gun store, your reaction to the gun's recoil can be judged only during shooting. Fortunately, good training can help shooters of any physique learn to handle even heavy-hitting calibers accurately. Even then, there is a cutoff after which the time between shots is too long for reliable self defense, because too much time elapses while the shooter overcomes recoil and reacquires the sight picture to make another accurate shot.

Most indoor gun ranges rent a variety of the popular model handguns. This is an excellent way for new shooters to gauge their own reaction to the recoil of .38 Special, 9mm, .357 SIG, .40 S&W and .45 ACP guns and ammunition before investing hundred dollars in a handgun. After choosing a suitable self-defense caliber, the most important decision is the shooter's willingness to practice with the handgun. A gun that causes discomfort during shooting is a gun that will not be shot very much. Weapon unfamiliarity is a recipe for disaster in self-defense situations.

Reliability Comes First

Many different factors affect handgun reliability. Nonetheless, before one adopts a handgun for self defense, the reliability of that weapon must be determined. Beginning shooters can broadly assume that revolvers are more reliable than semi-automatics, in the sense that there's less to malfunction in the revolver's simpler operating cycle.

A store clerk explains different pistol choices.

Springfield Armory's EMP single-action pistol fits this hand well.

Also, revolvers will genreally fire any kind of ammunition, hollowpoint or otherwise, without fear of failure.

Those who favor the semi-automatic owe it to themselves to make an even more intensive study of the handgun they are considering buying. Look for reviews in gun magazines, especially seeking out information on reliability, gun malfunctions, and brands of ammunition tested in the weapon. A semi-automatic's reliability, while first a question of design and production standards, is also greatly affected by cleaning and maintenance, and by the particular model's ability to feed specific kinds of ammunition. A self-defense handgun must cycle high performance hollowpoint ammunition 100% of the time.

After buying a self-defense handgun, the buyer must test that weapon with the ammunition she plans to carry. Semi-automatic owners need to fire about 200 rounds of their defense ammunition through their handgun to guarantee flawless feeding of the ammunition into the chamber and reliable ejection of the empty case after the round is fired. If the testing produces multiple malfunctions, repeat the process with different ammunition, until you have found hollowpoint ammunition that always functions in your self-defense gun.

While this sounds expensive, in reality a well-designed semi-automatic loaded with high quality ammunition will nearly always function properly. The testing will in all likelihood go smoothly, and if it does not, problems should show up within the first 50 rounds, so the ammunition can be switched before 200 rounds of expensive ammunition has been fired. If nothing cycles reliably in the gun, you may need to visit the gunsmith for a bit of fine-tuning or trade it in on one that works flawlessly.

Revolver shooters should also test and occasionally practice with their defense ammunition to remain accustomed to its recoil and to be sure the firing pin strikes the primers with sufficient force to discharge the round.

Many serviceable handguns are available for purchase. The buyer's responsibility is to select one with which she can safely train and practice. The gun needs to be concealable (if the owner intends to carry it outside the home) and must have adequate safety features to assure it will not be unintentionally discharged. Very low-budget semi-autos often lack firing pin blocks to prevent the hammer from striking the firing pin unless the trigger is pulled. These guns may discharge if an impact bounces the firing pin forward to strike the ammunition. Read up on the gun you intend to buy, and ask the gun store clerk about the internal safeties in the model you are considering. If a cheap gun that is not drop-safe is all you can afford, you are better off buying a less expensive used revolver.

This double feed malfunction occurred after the gun failed to extract the empty case and tried to feed a loaded cartridge into the chamber.

These are serious questions. *One of the easiest ways to find the answers is to postpone a handgun purchase until after you have completed at least a basic handgun training course.* Your basic training should put you in touch with qualified professionals who can help you solve gun selection puzzles. Study first, buy later.

Getting to Know Your Gun

Cleaning your handgun is an excellent way to better understand how it functions. A gun is an emergency rescue tool for which you bear an intense responsibility. If it malfunctions, you must understand how to correct the problem immediately and get back in the gun fight. A thorough understanding of its operation is crucial.

Initially, you'll need to ask the clerk selling you the gun to take a few uninterrupted minutes to show you how to take the gun apart and clean it. You have just handed over hundreds of dollars for this purchase. Don't be shy about asking for this small service before you walk out the door with your new gun. Another reference resource is the owner's manual, which usually includes a section on cleaning the weapon.

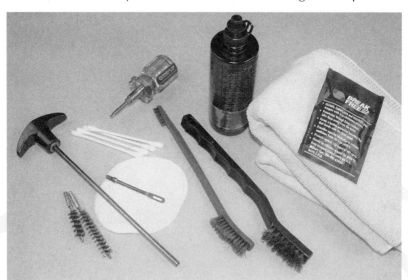

Gun cleaning supplies you'll need include chamber and or bore brushes, a cleaning rod, patch tip, cleaning patches, cotton swabs, a high quality gun screwdriver, nylon and metal brushes, gun cleaner, and soft, absorbent cloths.

Instructor Jim Jacobe oversees a gun cleaning session at his shooting school in Salem, OR.[4]

In addition, magazines that review guns sometimes include a description of how that gun is disassembled for cleaning. Over the years I have also made extensive use of the National Rifle Association's book *The NRA Guide to Pistols and Revolvers* and their *NRA Guide to Rifles and Shotguns*[3] for shotguns and rifles, too. I have gone so far as to put photocopied pages from this straightforward source of disassembly and reassembly directions in my cleaning kit, while learning the inner workings of my Remington shotguns and AR-15 rifle.

When I bought my first gun, the clerk assembled a list of cleaning supplies, which I dutifully bought on his recommendation. I went home and for the next month or so cleaned my revolver after each practice session without realizing the cylinder could be removed for a more convenient and thorough cleaning. My first basic shooting class included instruction in gun cleaning, and I was thrilled to learn the easy, correct way to clean that gun. The lesson? Find an instructor who will help answer your gun cleaning questions and demonstrate that skill in the course curriculum.

Notes

[1] Grant Cunningham Custom Revolvers for Sport and Defense, http://www.grantcunningham.com 503-307-9746

[2] Glock grip reduction, Burns Custom Pistols, 700 NW Gilman, Issaquah, WA 98027, 425-391-3202.

[3] *The NRA Guide to Rifles and Shotguns Revised and Expanded, and The NRA Guide to Pistols and Revolvers*, NRA Publications, 11250 Waples Mill Rd., Fairfax, VA 22030, 800-672-3888.

[4] See www.jimjacobe.com for contact info and class schedules by this fine instructor.

CHAPTER 18

All About Handgun Ammunition

H andgun ammunition comes in so many varieties that the beginning shooter may feel overwhelmed by the task of selecting ammunition for self defense. It often falls to a clerk in the gun store to recommend ammunition to the first-time gun buyer. The men who worked at a now-defunct Seattle-area gun range are probably still snickering about the woman who asked for a box of Federal Hydra-Shoks by requesting the "cartridge that causes a great hydrostatic shock if it is fired into a body." The clerk grinned and replied, "Lady, that describes most of the ammunition behind this counter."

Oh, well. We all have to start somewhere! You see, that woman was me.

Selecting a defensive handgun caliber is an exercise in compromise, because in reality handguns are the least powerful of common defensive weaponry. If available, a rifle or shotgun would serve far better in most defense emergencies, yet the larger guns are rarely accessible beyond home, ranch or business locations. We carry handguns for convenience, mobility and legal concealed carry – not for superior ballistics. When choosing a handgun for home or self defense, caliber is one of the first variables addressed, for confined to its limited power, we earnestly pursue the maximum effect reasonable.

Ammunition selection is a task complicated by the new shooter's ignorance of terms and vocabulary with which to communicate their needs, concerns and desires. Let us, then, begin with a little vocabulary session.

Ammunition Terminology

Ballistics: The science that deals with the motion of projectiles.

Cartridge: One unit of ammunition, composed of a bullet, a case, a primer and gunpowder (also called propellant). You will also hear the word "round" or "load" used informally to describe a cartridge of ammunition or a variety of ammunition.

Caliber: The diameter of the bullet at its base, measured in 100ths or 1000ths of an inch. Thus, a .22 caliber bullet is approximately 22/100ths of an inch in diameter; a .45 caliber bullet is approximately 45/100ths of an inch in diameter. Bullet diameter is also measured in millimeters. The European-born 9mm ammunition is a good example of bullet caliber expressed in metric units: its bullet is 9mm wide at its widest point (around .356"). Note that the caliber designation of many cartridges is a product of marketing rather than of actual measurement. For example, the .38 Special bullet actually has a caliber of about .356", not .38".

In general terms, caliber refers to the diameter of the bullet and the bore of the gun it will be fired through.

Bullet: The projectile seated in the top of the case that is fired out of the gun barrel. Bullets come in a multitude of shapes for various uses. The most common are hollowpoint, roundnose and truncated cone, either lead or jacketed, plus lead semi-wadcutters and full wadcutters. Bullet weights also vary by intended use. (Note that the bullet is only one part of a cartridge – the projectile that exits the barrel of the gun. No matter what you may hear in the movies, "bullet" and "cartridge" do not mean the same thing.)

Bullet weight: Bullets are described first by caliber (diameter), then by weight. Bullet weight is measured in units called grains: 7000 grains = one pound. It is common to hear discussion of a .45 caliber 185-grain hollow point bullet, referring to a bullet weighing 185 grains that measures approximately .45 inches in diameter at its base.

Wadcutter: A cylinder-shaped lead bullet, some with flat ends on both top and bottom, others with a cavity hollowed out at the base. The bullet is seated flush with the top of the case and is used in revolvers for target shooting because it cuts nice, round holes in paper.

Semi-wadcutter: A bullet that resembles the wadcutter (hence its name) that tapers to a small, flat top and when loaded as part of a cartridge extends above the case mouth. It is used in both revolvers

Varied bullet types include (L-R) wadcutter, semi-wadcutter, round nosed and hollow point bullet with expanded bullet of same caliber shown at right.

and semi-automatic handguns as target and practice ammunition.

Roundnose: Also a variety of practice ammunition valued for its reliable feeding in semi-automatic handguns. It consists of a solid, round-nosed bullet, either jacketed or lead, and is less expensive than hollowpoint bullets. This is sometimes also colloquially referred to as "ball" ammunition.

Hollowpoint: Hollowpoints resemble a semi-wadcutter or roundnose bullet with a deep recess cut into the top of the bullet. The hollowed out section allows the bullet to expand to a mushroom-like shape when it hits tissue or a similar medium. The expansion increases the size of the projectile, causing a larger wound channel and more tissue disruption for quicker physical incapacitation. This is the bullet you should carry for self defense unless prevented from so doing by law. Not only can hollowpoints cause quicker physical incapacitation, they are designed to stop inside the body of the assailant, dramatically reducing the danger that your bullet will go all the way through the assailant's body then hit an innocent bystander.

FMJ: Full metal jacket (FMJ) ammunition consists of a lead projectile fully encased in a copper jacket. This ammunition is free of the lubricant found on lead ammunition since the copper jacket slips easily through the gun's barrel when fired. Since there is no lubricant to burn, it produces considerably less smoke when fired, and because the lead bullet is enclosed in the jacket, it reduces lead exposure substantially. Semi-jacketed bullets leave the tip bare to aid in hollow-point expansion, especially at lower velocities.

Case: The metal cylinder and base that holds the gunpowder, bullet and primer. Cases are generally made of brass, but also steel and one-use disposable aluminum. While the strength of the case is important, it is the firearm's chamber that supports the case wall and keeps the case from rupturing while the burning powder is building up pressure to push the bullet out of the top of the case.

Primer: In a centerfire cartridge such as the .38 Special, the primer is a small round "cap" seated in an indentation in the base of the case which, when struck by the handgun's firing pin, sparks to ignite the gunpowder inside the case. The primer's function could be compared to an automobile spark plug. In a rimfire cartridge such as the .22LR, the primer is contained within the rim of the cartridge case, out of sight.

Powder: Also called propellant. Gunpowder, when ignited by the primer's spark, burns rapidly, building gas volume and pressure inside the case until the bullet is forced out the barrel of the gun at great velocity (usually around the speed of sound). The proportion of powder to airspace in the case, as well as its chemical composition, influences the pressures that build up while the powder burns and thus the velocity

Dent from the firing pin is seen on the empty rimfire case (left) while the unfired cartridge to the right is still intact.

Cartridge components include the primer, case, propellant (or powder), and the projectile (or bullet).

at which that pressure pushes the bullet through the gun barrel and out the muzzle.

ACP, S&W, Luger and Parabellum: These are caliber designations that give credit to the inventor of the particular caliber ammunition in question or its intended use. Examples: .380 ACP or .45 ACP = .380 Auto Colt Pistol, .45 ACP = .45 Auto Colt Pistol; .40 S&W = .40 Smith & Wesson; 9mm Luger (named after its designer, Georg Luger) or 9mm Parabellum ("Parabellum" means "for war" in Latin). The 9mm Luger and 9mm Parabellum are exactly the same size, and both can be fired through any 9mm Parabellum or Luger handgun. However, 9mm Kurz, 9mm Corto, and 9mm Short are multi-lingual terms used to describe .380 ACP ammunition chambered for a .380 ACP semi-auto pistol, and they are shorter than 9mm Parabellum or 9mm Luger in overall length. Similarly, .32 H&R Magnum ammunition is for .32 caliber revolvers and is radically different from .32 ACP auto cartridges.

Velocity: The speed at which the bullet travels is measured in feet per second. Thus, on boxes of "high performance" ammunition, you may find an estimate of how fast the bullet travels when fired. For instance on a high velocity .45 ACP caliber, the bullet weight may be stated as "185 grains," followed by "1150 fps," indicating that when fired from a 5-inch long barrel, the bullet was ripping along at 1150 feet per second when it left the muzzle.

Velocity is determined by how much pressure builds up in the case as the gunpowder burns, the weight of the bullet and the length of the barrel of the handgun. Smaller, lighter bullets travel faster, and according to some, higher velocities cause greater shock and tissue disruption in an assailant, bringing faster incapacitation.

+P or +P+, Subsonic and Magnum: Subsonic ammunition expels the bullet at speeds under 1000 feet per second, approximately the speed of sound at sea level. +P indicates ammunition designed to generate higher pressures than standard ammunition, and +P+ is a very high pressure load. Magnum ammunition, best known in the .357 and .44 Magnum calibers, builds enormous pressures before the bullet is

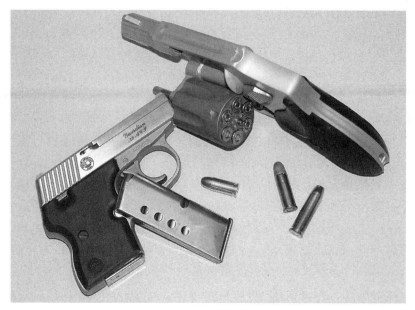

The .32 H&R Magnum (right) is a revolver cartridge, while the .32 ACP (left) is for semi-autos like the North American Arms Guardian shown. Both are .32 caliber, but the case length is significantly different, as is the rim, so they are not interchangeable.

expelled. Thus, one of our highest-pressure handgun cartridges, a .357 Magnum cartridge, for example, may have a bullet velocity from 1350 to 1450 feet per second. That's around 950 miles per hour!

What Is Stopping Power?

Let's begin by defining the terms that are loosely bandied around in this debate. The most ill-defined phrase, yet one with which we must contend, is "stopping power." For our purposes, we might do well to replace the phrase "stopping power" with "rapid incapacitation." In a self-defense emergency, even temporary incapacitation may be enough to allow the armed citizen to escape or to assert control.

Incapacitation in a gun fight occurs if the central nervous system is damaged or if bleeding diminishes blood pressure and blood flow to the brain. Sometimes, I tell students that they need to disrupt "electrical or plumbing," that is, the nervous or circulatory systems.

Location of the gunshot wound plays a vital role, as does, to a
lesser degree, the energy of the bullet. A great debate rages whether
permanent wounding is the method by which incapacitation occurs, or
whether the effect of the temporary wound channel (or stretch cavity)
occurring during the bullet's passage through tissue and the concurrent
shock effect is the factor causing physical shutdown.

While I don't expect to solve the stopping power debate, I respect
the compilation of results occurring during and after real-life shootings,
many involving police officers. These are collected by Evan Marshall,
and contained in two volumes he co-authored with engineer Ed
Sanow. If wishing to study more, obtain *Handgun Stopping Power: The
Definitive Study and Street Stoppers, and The Latest Handgun Stopping
Power Street Results* from Paladin Press.[1]

We use the terms "muzzle velocity" and "terminal velocity" to
describe projectile speed at the beginning and the end of the bullet's
flight. A handgun cartridge's self-defense potential, however, relies
heavily on the energy the bullet delivers, and that requires much more
than pure speed, which brings us to the term "momentum."

*Two examples of Magnums: the .44 Magnum and .44 Special (left) and .357
Magnum and the .38 Special, which share the same diameter but differ in
over all length.*

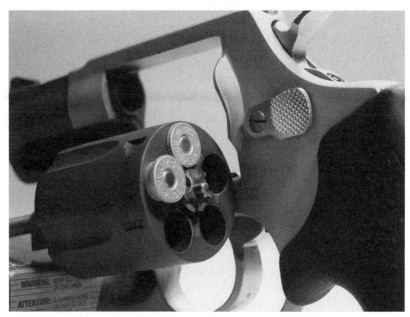

In a .38 Special revolver, the longer (and more powerful) .357 Magnum cartridge (lower) prevents the cylinder from closing and thus cannot be fired, though the shorter .38 Special (top) fits perfectly in the gun chambered for it. Being shorter but with an identical case width, the .38 Special can be fired in a .357 Magnum revolver, but not the other way around. The same is true of .44 Magnum and .44 Special ammunition.

Momentum is quantified as the bullet's mass in pounds (7000 grains = 1 lb.) multiplied by its velocity (in feet per second). When restricted to non-hollowpoint bullets, momentum is second only to shot placement as the crucial factor in handgun ammunition performance. Additional equations quantify the actual kinetic energy delivered by discharged ammunition, determined by multiplying the mass of the bullet times .5 the square of its velocity. Both "momentum" and "energy" are ways to describe the power of a cartridge of ammunition. Equations alone are not sufficient data upon which to make a choice about ammunition for self defense. Without the design characteristics of the hollowpoint or expanding bullet, the projectile can go and go and go – through the primary target and beyond without transferring all the energy into the target.

Bullet Performance

This brings us to bullet design. Along with bullet weight and velocity, shape, design, and even material composition of the projectile govern how it behaves when it strikes a consistent medium. Fortunately, at least as of this writing, most readers have the choice of hollowpoint bullets. Hollowpoints, the subject of much misinformation, have existed since the 1800s if not before.

In the 1960s and 1970s, ammunition manufacturers combined the idea of high velocity handgun ammunition with the hollowpoint bullet, showing that hollowpoints would expand more reliably if their velocity exceeded 1000 feet per second. Hollowpoint expansion prevents over-penetration and forces the bullet to expend its energy inside the target, with none wasted beyond. In this single development, handgun ammunition technology took a gigantic step forward, to the great benefit of smaller calibers like the 9mm Parabellum.

High velocity lightweight jacketed hollowpoints increase the likelihood of rapid incapacitation with smaller calibers like the .38 Special and 9mm Parabellum. The effect on .357 Magnum, .40 S&W and .45 ACP is to supercharge already decent handgun calibers by increasing velocity in the momentum equation.

Not one of the stopping power theoreticians can truthfully predict shooting results with 100% reliability. For one thing, although we evaluate ammunition in ordnance type gelatin, in real life, body construction varies from lean to obese, and bullets may strike solid bone. Other considerations include barriers ranging from bare skin in hot weather to a heavy leather jacket in cooler conditions, and incapacitation is further hindered by physiological factors including drug use and adrenaline or psychological conditions like dementia.

Making a Choice

If the mission is defending self and family, stopping power will rely on shot placement, bullet design and momentum. Using this guideline, few self-defense instructors will recommend cartridges in calibers

The expanded hollowpoint has considerably greater frontal surface, compared to the unfired example of the same bullet (right).

below .380 ACP, because the projectile lacks sufficient mass to do its part in the momentum equation. Handgun cartridges cannot produce pressures sufficient to compensate with pure velocity, as does the rifle ammunition we will discuss in a later chapter.

On this controversial topic, can we agree that beyond shot placement, stopping power largely depends on bullet momentum coupled with the hollowpoint's expansion into a larger frontal profile? To exploit all available energy, we can next conclude that larger calibers should cause quicker incapacitation. However, incapacitation primarily results from damage to the circulatory or nervous system, taking us back to the importance of accurate shot placement. A peripheral wound to a muscle group like the upper arm or thigh, even with a .357 Magnum, will not incapacitate a criminal as well as gunshots to the central torso where the heart and spine are located.

The handgun and caliber you choose should be sufficiently controllable that you can learn to accurately deliver quick, multiple shots. Otherwise, you simply have a tool, without the skills to make it work. Like driving a high-performance automobile with minimal skill, inadequate training makes handgun possession a real liability.

A good test of your ability to use a handgun in self defense is the "5 in 5 at 5" test I used when writing gun reviews. Position a five-inch circle target at five yards. Load the gun. If you don't have a shot timer, have a friend time you, saying, "Go," and at the end of five seconds, yelling, "stop!" If you have fired five rounds inside the five-inch radius in five seconds at the practical self-defense distance of five yards, you have likely found a gun you can use effectively for self defense.

Bigger Is Better – Up to a Point

Perceptive readers have already noted that although we have argued the defense potential and shortcomings of smaller calibers, nothing has been said about the very large handgun calibers like .41 Magnum, .44 Magnum, and .50 AE or the remaining variety of large .40 to .50 caliber hunting handgun calibers. These magnums and the 10mm recoil viciously and will slow your shot-to-shot times.

Besides producing punishing recoil, the very large handgun calibers require a larger framed gun, and this alone disqualifies them for the many who will legally carry a concealed pistol. Reasonable self-defense caliber choices, when partnered with modern hollowpoint ammunition, include the .380 ACP, .38 Special, 9mm Parabellum, .357 Magnum, .357 SIG, .40 S&W, .44 Special and .45 ACP.

No Magic Bullet

There is no magic bullet. Accurate shot placement is of utmost importance. The most viable target is the center of the chest at armpit level. This increases the chances of a heart, lung or spinal cord hit. In addition, a center-of-mass aim point is quickest and most reliable for the adrenaline-filled defender. Students of armed self defense must learn to shoot until the threat ceases. Unless the spinal cord is severed or the brain's medulla oblongata hit, the assailant may be capable of continued hostilities after taking several handgun bullets. You must be capable of repeated, accurate shots to the center of the assailant's chest.

Misses don't count in a gunfight, and in the end, your life is the prize.

Notes

[1]Marshall, Evan, and Sanow, Ed, *Street Stoppers, The Latest Handgun Stopping Power Street Results* and *Handgun Stopping Power: The Definitive Study*. Paladin Press, Gunbarrel Tech Center, 7077 Winchester Circle, Colorado 80301, 800-466-6868, 800-392-2400.

CHAPTER 19

Shooting Skills

E arlier we discussed obtaining basic handgun training and understanding appropriate use of deadly force. During subsequent chapters, we have emphasized the importance of accurate shot placement. Marksmanship skills are just the beginning; your training needs to include learning to shoot accurately and rapidly despite the distractions and stress of a self-defense emergency.

Remember, you cannot learn to shoot or safely use a gun by reading a book. You must find qualified instructors who will help you give physical form to the ideas we discuss here. In basic handgun class you should have learned about gun safety, sight picture, follow-through and trigger control. To reiterate anything you may have forgotten or did not completely understand, here is an overview of the basics.

Dry Firing

Dry firing – the simulated firing of an empty, unloaded gun – can be a valuable training technique. You don't need to go to the range to practice a smooth, controlled trigger pull, speed reloads, or draw and dry fire skills. Champion pistol shooters all practice dry fire because despite one's level of skill, flinching – that near-instinctive reaction to loud noise and violent motion – is an unavoidable human physiological response to extensive live firing. Dry fire is the cure to the flinch, and it's inexpensive because it requires no ammunition. It is also practical: with planning, you can do it almost anywhere, provided you follow stringent safety procedures. Best of all, it lets you ingrain a perfect trigger pull without the aversive stimuli of the gun firing, so the practice habituates the body to pull the trigger smoothly without flinching.

Dry fire practice, however, is a two-edged sword. Valuable because it is without question the best way to develop trigger control, dry fire is dangerous unless performed under very stringent safety rules. This may be the reason nearly every gun manufacturer warns against the practice.

With rimfire guns, like a .22 LR pistol or rifle, the warning stems from potential damage to the gun itself, which can be avoided through the use of Snap Caps to protect the firing pin and the edges of the chamber.[1] On shotguns and rifles, too, there is potential for accelerated wear to the firing pin. Snap Caps or other inert dummy cartridges are recommended as a way to avert mechanical problems, yet these, too, are not without risk because live and dummy ammunition may be inadvertently mixed up. With centerfire handguns, including most self-defense pistols, the manufacturer's warning is rooted in safety and liability concerns.

Dry fire entails all the steps of discharging a gun with one crucial difference: the absence of ammunition. In one careless moment, live ammunition may all too easily be loaded in the gun during a dry fire practice session. Danger of a negligent discharge and the subsequent liability are behind manufacturer's warnings against dry firing. Those dangers are very real and should not be ignored.

Sight Picture

The handgun has two sighting devices to help you align the barrel with your target. The front sight is generally a blade with serrations, a dot or colored insert to help you see it clearly. The rear sight is a notch shaped like a squared-off letter "U" and may have two dots or a bright outline around the notch to mark the edges in poor light. As you look through the rear sight, if the front sight is perfectly centered in the notch of the rear sight and the tops of both front and rear sights are perfectly aligned at the moment the gun discharges, the bullet will hit the part of the target covered by the front sight. This arrangement is called "combat sights" and is common on most service pistols. Target pistols, guns designed purely for sporting pursuits, may use a slightly different arrangement regulated so the bullet strikes the target right above the front sight at a specified distance; this arrangement is called "target sights." For self defense, we prefer the former, since it is impossible to predict self defense distances.

As we aim the gun at the target we see three objects: the rear sight, the front sight and the target beyond. When all three are viewed in

Focus the eye on the front sight and let the target and rear sight go blurry.

alignment, it is called the "sight picture." If we focus our vision on the rear sight, anything beyond it is blurry. If we see the target clearly, both front and rear sight will be too fuzzy to keep them lined up accurately. Like a simple camera, our eyes can focus on only one visual plane at a time. We must concentrate on only the front sight to be sure our sights remain aligned, with the front sight covering the place we wish the bullet to strike.

On paper targets, or facing an assailant, it is natural to want to look at the object we intend to shoot. That creates a problem, because focusing on the target allows the front sight to move out of alignment, causing inaccuracy. Allow the target to go slightly blurry. Focus your vision on the front sight as if it holds your life and your future.

Trigger Squeeze

A smooth, consistent pressure on the trigger is the key to accurate shooting. Jerking the trigger moves the sights out of alignment, making the shot go wild. This happens right at the end of the trigger pull, and many novice shooters are not aware that they have moved the sights so radically until they notice how far off center their hit is located. Just as experienced drivers press the car brake pedal smoothly until they bring the vehicle to a stop, on a smaller scale, that same smooth control is what you want from your trigger finger.

Physical skills are best learned slowly. Mastery is the result of precise performance of the actions required, first at a slow pace, then with tiny, incremental increases in speed as the motion is refined. Thus, a deliberate four-second trigger squeeze starts with up to three seconds of smooth controlled pressure on the trigger. At some point between two and four seconds, the gun fires (sometimes described as the shot breaking or the hammer falling), although the skilled shooter does not try to predict the exact instant the discharge will occur. The remaining time is dedicated to follow-through: bringing the gun back on target, lining up the sights and assessing the situation to see if you need to shoot again, all before releasing the trigger. The same consistent trigger press, surprise hammer fall and subsequent shot break, and follow through can be compressed to well under a second per shot as your skills grow. Consistent, smooth trigger pressure without anticipation of the shot is the key component in effective trigger manipulation at any speed.

Make It A Surprise

Why should we be surprised when the gun goes off? Obviously, if the finger is pressing the trigger, we should expect the gun to fire. The surprise I'm talking about is not being so focused on the progress of the trigger pull that I can predict the exact instant in which the gun will fire.

Again, why? Were you surprised by the noise and jolt in your hand the first time you fired a handgun? I think we all were. Our bodies said, "That's threatening, let's find a way to avoid it next time." Even though our minds know we can survive this aversive stimulus, the body instinctively shies away. If you know exactly when the gun is going to fire, your body will flinch away as it tries to escape the recoil and noise. The flinch or jerking movement pulls the sights off target and the bullet goes astray. However, if you do not know precisely when the gun is going to fire, there is no flinching, anticipatory reaction. Let each shot break as a surprise.

The last sentence is a lot like saying, "Stop your eyes from blinking," because the flinch happens on a reflexive level. Not knowing when the gun is going to fire is the only way to prevent the reflexive reaction to the aversive stimuli of recoil and noise. Obviously, even a young child can figure out at what point in the trigger pull the discharge occurs, so good shooters trick themselves into ignoring that critical moment.

A good drill to improve trigger control is called ball and dummy, in which the revolver shooter randomly loads two or three of the chambers in her revolver, leaving the others empty. Closing the cylinder without observing the order in which the cartridges will fire, we go on to shoot a slow-fire exercise. When the firing pin goes into an empty chamber, you can observe any flinching reaction that disrupts sight picture, because the sight picture should still be there after the hammer falls, since there is no recoil with dry fire! Using dummy cartridges like Saf-T-Trainers[1] gives semi-auto shooters the opportunity to practice the same valuable drill with the added benefit of getting in some practice clearing failure-to-fire malfunctions.

Like bowling or golf, follow-through is critical to accurate shot placement. Follow-through with a firearm consists of realigning the sights on target after the recoil of the shot disrupts the sight picture. The sights are realigned on target before the trigger is released. Even if you know a second shot is not needed (in competition, for example) the discipline of a complete follow-through keeps the shooter from raising her head to look at the target while the shot goes off. When the shooter

She's only going to load three rounds positioned randomly, so this shooter can work on trigger control drills using the ball and dummy exercise.

peeks at the target, sight alignment is lost at the critical moment the gun fires, sacrificing accuracy. In self defense, follow-through prepares the handgun and the shooter to make an accurate second shot if the threat remains.

Stance Builds Power

Still having some misses? Check your stance and your grip. Because a handgun recoils with each shot fired, a rock-firm grip is needed to maintain control and to keep the sight picture precise for consecutive shots. The dominant hand grasps the gun grip panels with the hand's web pressed firmly into the grip tang at the top of the back strap. Grasping the gun low on the grips allows the muzzle to rise unnecessarily during recoil. For maximum control, hold as high on the grips as you can, with the fleshy web of your hand blocking the gun's rearward recoil. The support hand wraps over the firing hand, like a tight fist on top of another fist. Support-hand fingers press atop the firing hand knuckles, and the non-firing hand's thumb sits right on top of the firing hand's thumbnail and locks down, pushing the thumbs in against the gun.

A good shooting grip needs the support of strong, balanced footing in the same way a house needs a good foundation to withstand strong winds. For beginners, the Isosceles stance is inherently the strongest and fastest to assume. The Isosceles stance is based on feet positioned shoulder-width apart, with arms and wrists simply locked straight out for fast, accurate firing.

The foundation of any range shooting stance is foot position. Feet must be placed an immodest shoulder width apart for balance and stability. Women students, especially those of mature ages, find this the most unnatural part of shooting. Women have excellent hand-eye coordination and can manipulate the little safety levers and magazine release buttons well, yet standing with their feet wide for balance is disconcerting, going against all their socialization. People trained in a martial art are generally more comfortable in a wide stance, knowing they're vulnerable to knockdown attacks if they keep their feet together. Before aiming the gun, check that your feet are at least as wide as your shoulders and are not aligned as if walking a tightrope (see diagram).

So, let's review the Isosceles stance: Starting from the feet up, the feet are at least shoulder width apart and toes point toward the target. Not only is this a natural stance, it accommodates movement, which is essential in a real-life emergency. The leg on the firing-hand side is placed to the rear with a very slight bend at the knee. The non-dominant side leg is forward and flexes at the knee to act as a shock absorber against the gun's recoil. Flex both knees, because locked joints create a pivot point from which recoil or a blow will steal your balance. The hips face the target straight on, with the derrière tucked forward. The shoulders likewise face the target squarely. Arms are locked straight out, punching the gun toward the target. The head may tuck down into the shoulders a little, a natural response to this aggressive, body-forward posture.

For maximum control on a hard-kicking handgun, the author prefers the old-fashioned grip shown here with thumbs locked one atop the other to keep the hands together.

The aggressive Isosceles stance is a fast and stable shooting platform.

The Ready Position

If the assailant runs away but you aren't sure the entire area is safe, you may need to escape, get out of the immediate area or go to call for help. In the wake of a deadly force threat, you will want the gun readily available in your hands, yet protected from a gun grab should a hidden accomplice be waiting. The gun also needs to be out of your line of vision so you can scan for additional threats. These concerns prevent stalking around with the gun in a fully extended shooting stance.

Instead, maintain your strong, two-handed grip on the decocked or on-safe gun and tuck your elbows back against your ribs, trigger finger indexed on the frame of the gun, well away from the trigger guard, and

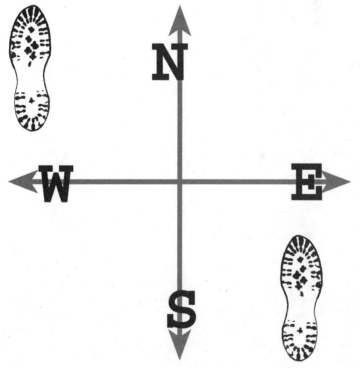

Diagram illustrates the wide, squared-off foot position that lends the Isosceles stance its strength. As shown, if facing north, the right-handed shooter's right foot it back in the southeast quadrant, their left foot is well forward in the northwest quarter. Lefties stand opposite.

point the muzzle down about two feet in front of your feet. We call this the low ready position.

Hold the gun close to your torso, out of reach of an assailant who may try to disarm you, while keeping it instantly ready to punch out into a shooting stance. Gripped thus, the gun is in the strongest

Jacqueline demonstrates the safe low ready position in which we hold the unholstered gun while not shooting.

retention position possible. When hand and arm strength is required, it is difficult to exert power at arms' length. For example, to open a sealed jar, we hunker down and concentrate our strength at the center of the body.

The Hollywood high ready, with the gun pointing up, is only a cinematic technique to include the gun in the film frame with the actor's face. It has little tactical advantage and just cries out for a disarm attempt.

Gun Handling Skills

After you have mastered basic sight picture, grip, and stance, you need to refine your skills to keep the gun loaded and firing during combat or competition. Safe speed reloads are important, as is the ability to correct any malfunction of the weapon. You should have one primary reloading technique: a speed reload. Don't allow yourself to

A gun held close to the body's centerline is more easily defended from a gun grab than one held at arm's length.

ingrain sloppy reloading habits while shooting for fun or during slow fire practice. The motions you make during fun and practice are those you will repeat under stress.

The late Jim Cirillo, who survived a number of gunfights during his stint with the New York City Police Department Stake Out Squad, told me of several incidents in which officers repeated gun handling sequences that had been unintentionally incorporated in their formal training. Some years ago, he related, the revolver-armed officers were trained to shoot a course of fire, then unload their empty brass cases into a can provided for that purpose. They were then to reload and shoot again. The officers were sent to the training range with 100 rounds in their pockets and were not sent to the training line with speed loaders or dump pouches. Reports from on-duty shootings

With the gun held at face level, she has little strength with which to combat a disarming attempt.

told of police officers who shot at assailants until their revolvers were empty, then turned and looked for the brass can while still under attack, according to Jim.

In an armed confrontation, the useless empties must be discarded immediately, new ammunition inserted and the gun brought back up on target in a matter of seconds. From the comfort of your easy chair, you may be tempted to say, "Of course, I already knew that." But on the range, do you catch your revolver's empty cases tidily in your hand? Do you carefully withdraw your $60 semi-auto magazine before it can fall to the ground and become scratched? Every practice reload should be treated as if it is training for a life-threatening confrontation – because it is.

Speed reloads with the semi-auto can be practiced at home, with the gun's slide and barrel removed and magazines inserted only into the frame. Disassemble the frame from the slide, then practice over a bed or couch to buffer the magazine's fall. The disassembled gun removes the danger of handling a fireable gun in an unsecured area. Alternatively, Brownells sells the Safety Mag, a solid synthetic replica of magazines for a half-dozen popular types of semi-auto pistols. Its use accommodates cycling the slide after a dryfire reload, but for safety, it must only be used where no loaded magazines are available.

Live-fire Practice Routines

Just like your smooth trigger pull, clearing malfunctions is a habituated skill, and one more crucial to the semi-auto shooter. Revolver shooters simply give the trigger another pull and hope the fault was in the ammunition, not the gun. Semi-auto shooters can reinforce speed and ability to clear semi-automatic malfunctions on the range using dummy cartridges. Produced by Precision Gun Specialties, and sold by Brownells[2] the bright orange Saf-T-Trainer dummy rounds can be interspersed with live rounds in a magazine, simulating a failure to fire. When a trigger pull produces a click instead of bang, the student performs a failure-to-fire malfunction clearance drill.

Load several magazines at random, mixing in three or four dummy rounds with the live ammunition. Have a friend load the magazines, or mix several magazines until you cannot anticipate in what order the live and dummy rounds will come. The element of surprise makes the training realistic. Along with rapidly performing the clearance drill, watch your front sight during the dummy round's trigger pull to observe any flinching caused by anticipating the shot. Making the conscious connection between your flinch and what happens to sight alignment when you flinch is a valuable training epiphany. Attaining this realization, the shooter is able to feel the flinch building before it happens and redouble attention on making a smooth trigger pull and surprise hammer fall.

As the empty magazine is released from the pistol, the shooter's hands have already accessed a loaded magazine from the belt pouch in which she carries it.

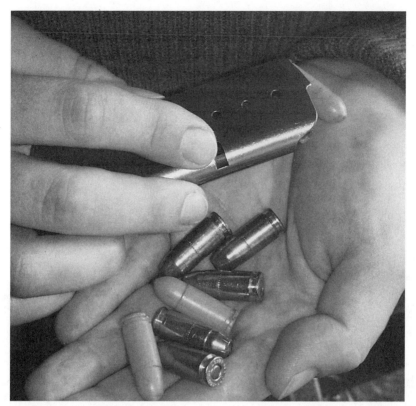

Randomly loading live ammunition and Saf-T-Trainers into a semi-automatic magazine, this shooter prepares to practice both malfunction clearing and trigger control.

Malfunction drills are a valuable part of your practice and training. Clearing malfunctions increases your understanding of how your gun works and increases your gun-handling capability. Repeating clearance drills imprints the correct motions on your mind, and should the weapon malfunction during a class or a match, you will be gratified by a skilled, smooth response that puts your hands in motion to get the gun back in the game. More important, if the gun fails on the street, your rapid, trained reaction, performed while moving to cover, may save your life. In addition, reloading, drawing and trigger control drills can be performed with Airsoft pistols, realistic spring- and air-powered faux firearms that shoot small plastic pellets.

When you go shooting with friends or practice alone, make the accuracy of each round fired of paramount importance. Take care to avoid making poor technique a habit. Even when shooting just for fun, shoot with a strong grip, stance, and precise sight alignment. If shooting with others, set up a friendly competition with some kind of stakes. Every shot outside the X ring can "cost" a quarter's donation to a charity or an organization like your area's grass roots gun rights lobby. With shooters of varying skills, establish a handicap, like the more skilled shooter firing left-handed to make it truly competitive.

Notes

[1]Saf-T-Trainers and Snap Caps sold by Brownells, 200 S. Front St., Montezuma, IA 50171, 515-623-4000, www. brownells.com

[2]Ibid.

SIG Sauer's Airsoft pistols are used in scenarios taught to help students grasp proper tactics against an armed attacker.

CHAPTER 20

Concealed Carry

The "art" of concealed carry is more complex than stuffing a revolver in your handbag or in the waistband of your jeans! Newcomers to the world of armed self defense are dazzled by the array of holsters, gun bags, and other carry devices marketed. The topic is one of such depth and breadth that it deserves its own large book, but until that work can be attempted, let's cover the high points about how to carry a concealed self-defense gun.

There exists no utterly comfortable way to wear a concealed handgun. The best we can hope for, primarily, is complete concealment of the gun. Comfort can be fine tuned with different holsters, maybe even using various models of one brand of handgun for various situations. Winter clothing will accommodate a larger, generally higher capacity handgun than the lighter garb of summer. Two guns, one large, the other small, with comparable locations for safety and magazine releases can make it easier to carry a gun all the time.

Unfortunately, it may take several purchases to find the right holster for you and your gun. Nearly every gun owner I know jokes about wanting to have a holster garage sale. Like me, they own several holsters per gun, some they know they will never use because they looked more functional than experience proved them to be. The following principles may keep new gun owners from spending money and accumulating way too many holsters in an attempt to find one that works.

Start with the Basics

Among experienced armed citizens, the primary holster choice for concealed handgun carry is generally some variety of belt holster. Many women have tried holsters made for men and given up prematurely on the idea of using a belt holster. Before you admit defeat, try one of the belt holsters made specifically for women from makers like Kramer Handgun Leather[1], Blade-Tech[2], Mitch Rosen[3], Rusty Sherrick[4], FIST Holsters[5], or Matt Del Fatti[6]. Other women have found the cross-draw holster is a good belt rig alternative.

Like any other personal-safety issue, learning to wear a holstered gun and becoming accustomed to its presence is not altogether easy. It takes effort, patience and ingenuity. A belt and holster place some restraints on your wardrobe. Casual garb is more likely to accommodate a belt and holster with minimal fuss. Until I began using a tailor, I fought suits on which the trousers belt loops were too small for the belt that fits most of my holsters.

There are numerous belt holster variations, but you should insist on one with a rigid mouth that remains open after the gun is drawn.

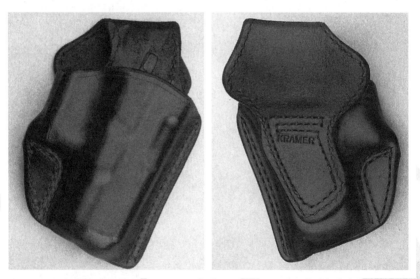

Kramer Handgun Leather's women's holster uses an extended belt loop to position the gun lower on a woman's body.

The precision fit of belt, holster and magazine pouch from one holster maker is best, as seen with this set from John Ralston's 5-Shot Leather.

Mitch Rosen's women's holster cants the muzzle forward of the hip.

Blade Tech's dropped and offset holster.

Rusty Sherrick suggests a cut down the front of the holster to make it easier to draw the gun.

Jim Murnack at FIST holsters has ingeniously duplexed Kydex® and leather in a handsome holster that is both thin and rigid.

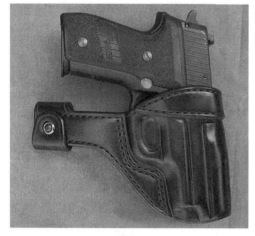

Matt DelFatti uses a long belt loop extension at the back of his holster to pull the gun's grips away from a woman's ribs.

Sometimes, a spring steel band will be enclosed in leather to keep the holster open for safe, one-handed holstering. Other holsters rely on very stiff construction, like Greg Kramer's premium-quality horsehide holsters or Jim Murnack's duplexed Kydex and leather holsters.

This is an important feature should you find it necessary to hold an assailant at gun point. What will the police perceive when they come on the scene? How will they know you are the victim, not the assailant? Trust me, the gun in your hand marks you as an unidentified threat to officers responding to your call. You can avoid a mistaken-identity shooting by discretely holstering the gun the moment before officers arrive. The rigid, open top allows you to holster the gun without looking, so you can keep your eyes on the assailant. Rigid nylon holsters, like the Bianchi[7] Accu-mold line, and gear made from other synthetic materials like Kydex approach the performance of leather and are often less expensive. You should, whatever the material, insist that the holster remain open at the top when the gun is drawn.

A Better Fit

For the womanly figure, I like a concealment holster positioned in what is called appendix carry, tucked in the concave curve between abdomen and strong-side hip. It was recommended to me when I was first carrying a five-shot revolver and when climate allowed an over shirt or vest to conceal the gun. I continued to use it when I carried the larger Glock 23. Although the gun seems obvious to the wearer in this position, it quite invisible to those not in on your secret.

For the same reason, cross draw holsters work well for women. A woman's figure is studied in the buttocks or bust line. The abdomen is not subject to that much scrutiny. Although care must be taken to do so safely, the appendix carry is very fast from which to draw and the

Small Kahr Arms PM9 simply disappears beneath a light shirt when carried just forward of the strong side hip.

only downside I discovered was that it required a closed vest or shirt to conceal it.

Women are substantially shorter through the torso than men. Recently, a 5'8" tall friend described trying out her husband's paddle holster. We laughed as she indicated the spot in her armpit to which she reported the grips of her Glock 23 extended, yet we were happy she hadn't paid $80 to buy the holster only to discover that men's high-rise holsters rarely are functional for women. One of my leading criteria in belt holster selection for women is a holster mouth must not sit any higher than the beltline.

Mitch Rosen's American Rear Guard holster is an excellent example of a very high quality holster that sits low inside the trouser waistband for the best-possible concealment. While many find an inside the waistband holster uncomfortable, Rosen's design eliminates many of the problems by angling the gun at an extreme cant. For several years, I carried a Heckler &Koch P7M8 in the Rear Guard, and it was so comfy that at times, I would check to see if I'd forgotten to put on the gun. It remains the only gun and holster I've ever worn that I could literally forget I had on. John Ralston's Inside Burton Scabbard has proven nearly as comfortable for the Springfield EMP I carry today. Not surprisingly, it also carries the gun at quite an angle directly behind my strong side hip.

In this mode of carry, one learns not to lean over in public, since the butt of even a small gun makes a recognizable outline even when covered by fabric. In the grocery store, for instance, I'll squat to pick up items on low shelves instead of just bending over to collect them. Choose a good quality holster from a reputable manufacturer. Readily available choices include Bianchi, Galco, Blade-Tech and DeSantis.[8] Spend a few more dollars and you can have the workmanship of a Milt Sparks, Rusty Sherrick, Greg Kramer, or Mitch Rosen rig.

Some holsters come outfitted to accommodate several widths of belts. My Milt Sparks Executive Companion, for instance, has two screws that attach the belt loop to the holster.[9] A smaller loop is sold

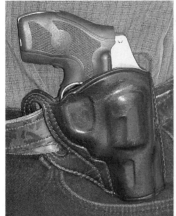

The cross draw holster, this one from Galco International, can hide the gun beneath a blouse or vest draping loosely from the bustline.

for 1-inch belts and costs $9, which I gladly spent, knowing some trousers wouldn't accommodate my inch-and-a-quarter gun belt. And speaking of belts, your common dress belt isn't going to last long under the weight of your gun and holster. Budget $90 to $125 for a rigid gun belt produced by a reputable holster manufacturer. A sturdy belt, like Galco's Contour Concealable, is critical to successful belt holster carry, as it eliminates most of the holster's movement.[10] The contour cut lets the belt snug to your curves with surprising comfort and having worn contour-cut belts for years, I cannot imagine why a woman would try to carry a holstered gun on anything else.

As the Internet brings smaller artisans into the public eye, I've discovered holster maker John Ralston of 5-Shot Leather[11], who crafted a belt, holster and magazine pouch set that incorporated a contour belt with thinner front section, the exact angle I prefer on the holster and other refinements individual to my needs. This kind of service is available for the asking and comes highly recommended.

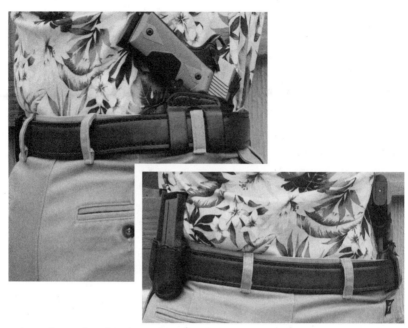

John Ralston of 5-Shot Leather custom fit this belt, holster and magazine pouch set to the author's needs. The belt has a contour cut, and the holster has just the right angle for comfort.

Learning to Wear It

The new concealed carry practitioner is uncomfortably aware of the gun and holster, especially during the break in period. It takes self-control to avoid fiddling with the gun, holster and clothing. In public you may only give the concealing garment a pat or pull when alone, upon standing up or getting out of a car or at other times when adjusting one's clothing would be normal without a holstered pistol. Press through this disturbing period by practicing concealed carry at first in privacy.

Not everyone is willing to endure the initial discomfort of breaking in and becoming accustomed to wearing an inside the waistband holster. Female figures, especially those with a tiny waistline and curving hips, may find an IWB intolerable, although a radical angle (cant) provides some relief. Usually, these more womanly figures find carrying in the appendix position their most comfortable option, or

*Author's daily conceal-
ment rig custom built
by 5-Shot Leather.*

Galco's Concealable Contour belt has proven both durable and comfortable.

they give up on IWB altogether. If wearing a belt scabbard on the outside of the trousers, you will need to exaggerate concealment techniques: rely on bulkier clothing, heavier fabrics, and roomier fashions. With a belt scabbard, the trouser fabric won't cover the bottom of the holster, so the covering garment must be considerably longer, too.

Alternatives to the Belt Holster

It takes a few years to replace ordinary garments with those that will accommodate your belt, holster and gun, so it might be good to start with more than one carry method, including a sturdy "belly band" that holds the gun tight against the torso with wide, Velcro®-secured elastic. Sources include DeSantis, Gould & Goodrich[12], Galco and other holster companies.

Another alternative to a belt-holstered gun is the shoulder holster. The majority of shoulder holsters sold will not conceal a defensive handgun on a woman's body, because it is carried horizontally and the muzzle extends beyond the back. Trust me, the distinctive outline of the muzzle or the tip of the holster can be mistaken for nothing but a shoulder holster – something everyone has seen repeatedly on TV cop dramas.

Invest the time and effort to shop for a vertical shoulder holster if this is an on-body carry method you favor. Choices from well-known manufacturers include Uncle Mike's[13] and Bianchi International. The gun is carried beneath the non-dominant arm with the muzzle pointing down and the pistol's grips forward. A good harness should distribute the weight of the pistol and spare ammunition. Concealment, of course, requires a jacket or loose over-garment, as well as some care that a collar covers the material of the harness.

My friend Jane, who introduced me to the Milt Sparks Executive Companion inside-the-waistband holster, carried her Glock in the traditional position, behind her strong side hip. She is taller and has a trimmer waistline than I, and her gun concealed comfortably in that position. Nonetheless, the last time I saw Jane, on a humid July day in western Washington, she was toting a .38 Special revolver in a waist-pack holster. Hot weather will be a determining factor in how you carry your gun. I also sometimes concede to hot weather by tucking my semi-automatic into a specially designed waist-pack. I prefer nylon to leather, since it has a more common appearance that does not announce "gun!" Some holster fanny packs have wide Velcro straps to secure the gun, an elastic band to hold an extra magazine in place, plus a cord for a downward rip to unzip the carry pouch and expose the gun for the draw. Others have a built-in holster attached to the back panel of the bag.

Choices include Bianchi's roomy nylon pouch with side pockets, an unusual detail I appreciated. I like a small pocket to serve exclusively as magazine pouch or place to tuck pistol permits and identification papers or other objects I don't want mixed with other things. DeSantis was the original designer to use Velcro on fanny pack pockets, a design they've patented. For years, I used their Gunnysack II, an extremely well-designed fanny pack with a full rip-away front panel that reliably exposes the holstered gun for a fast draw. I loved the bright colors in which it was made, since that made it just look like a tourist's pack.

Men do have it easier in a few regards. Not only do men's rest room

Holster alternative: the bellyband is versatile and lets you carry a gun under all kinds of clothing.

lines move faster, men don't have to give birth, and they can wear ankle holsters with nearly all of their trousers! An ankle holster is one of the hardest-to-detect modes of concealed carry. I'm always a little jealous as I watch my husband tuck his .38 Special airweight revolver into an ankle rig deeply concealed beneath his dark dress socks.

Women's fashions change every season. When slim-cut trousers are the rage, the ankle holster reverts to a gentleman's carry option. However, boot cut jeans, painter pants, straight-legged trousers and cuffed chinos will generally camouflage a tiny .380 ACP semi-auto carried in a trim elastic holster worn on the feminine ankle. While drawing from this method is a bit slow, and absolutely does not work while you are moving, it allows you to remain armed in an office where blouses and dress slacks are the daily uniform. Of course, you

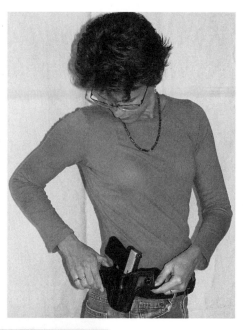

Joanna demonstrates the convenience of the snapping belt loops on her Alessi holster. This rig works well for her since the very short-barreled Kahr pistol it carries does not extend far below her belt line and so it is concealeable.

Vertical shoulder holster blends pistol's outline with torso of even a small woman.

Nylon holster waistpack blends with author's motorcycle gear and is quite unobtrusive there because many riders carry wallets and other essentials in waistpacks.

must sit carefully, avoiding crossed legs that expose the gun. An inch or two of extra length at the trouser hemline will assure that when you sit, the fabric will not ride up and reveal your handgun tucked on the inside of your calf right above the ankle bone. For better comfort, wear a thin stocking beneath the holster, then add a second thin stocking over the holster, pulling it up to the grips of the gun, but not over them.

Drawing your handgun from an ankle holster requires practice. The right-handed "defender" takes a big step, left-leg forward. The left hand lifts a handful of trouser leg on the thigh above the knee, where the hand can rest and support the weight as the right hand snakes down and snatches the gun from its holster on the inside the left ankle. The defender then simply straightens the torso enough to align the sights on target and is ready to shoot. The feet are already in an aggressive shooting stance. If the pants are too tight to grab and lift, drop to the non-gun knee, grab the pistol and shoot from a kneeling position.

North American Arms .380 Guardian carried in an ankle holster is sandwiched between two stockings for better concealment and comfort when the dress code makes it impossible to carry a larger gun at the waistline.

I have also carried in an ankle holster at business meetings all day, only to transfer the small .380 semi-auto to an empty coat pocket for a trip back to a motel room later that evening. Drawing from an ankle holster is never going to beat the speed of a gun in the hand, a consideration when riding the commuter train or walking through dark parking lots!

Holster Purses

I'm very uneasy with a gun carried off the body, but reality takes its toll on idealism, and I have to admit that there are times when a purse or holster bag is a reasonable option that will let some women keep a gun in easy reach. At a dress-up affair, a woman carrying a pretty sequined or beaded purse is inconspicuous, however a woman who cannot take off her jacket can become uncomfortable. I concede: a gun purse is a good solution under limited circumstances.

Some will ask why they can't carry a gun in their normal handbag. There are several very good reasons to only use a special bag designed as a holster. The first is the presence of other objects that become caught in and foul the gun's action, or worse yet, may disengage the gun's safety risking a negligent discharge. This is not just a problem for amateurs. I still remember my amazement, when attending an

American Society of Law Enforcement Trainers conference, as I listened to a trainer describe the tribulations of an off-duty female law enforcement officer who drew a revolver from her purse to find an eyebrow pencil jammed down the barrel.

The second reason for using a purse specially designed to carry a gun is drawing speed. Pulling a handgun from a conventional purse is terribly slow, as the defender fumbles with the latch or zipper, then dredges through the other personal effects trying to reach the weapon. A gun purse has a separate pouch that is inaccessible from the rest of the bag, often with a sewn-in holster to hold the gun in the same position all the time. At a minimum, this separation protects your gun

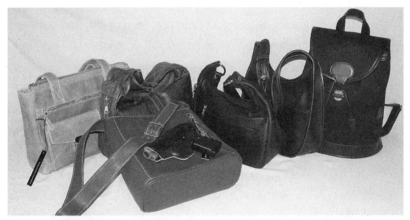

Attractive handbags from makers like Coronado Leather[14] and Galco feature separate compartments that contain a pistol holster.

Inside this Galco "Newport" gun purse, a special compartment just for the gun and its holster keeps other purse debris away from your defense gun.

from open view when you reach in to get your wallet, lipstick or other common purse contents. To draw, insert your hand, grasp the gun grips and present the weapon in a cross-draw manner. If the gun purse does not have a dedicated pouch and a built-in holster, don't buy it. There are plenty of very good gun purses that have built-in holsters and fast, positive closures that make getting to the gun quicker in an emergency.

The greatest difficulty I have in justifying gun purses is the question of proper response to a purse snatching. Experts agree that the best defense against muggers or purse snatchers is to give them the purse or wallet, so long as the woman is allowed to escape unharmed. A run-by purse snatching can turn into an ugly ground fight if the woman struggles to keep her bag. However, the good advice to give up a snatched bag is drastically altered by the presence of a deadly weapon in the purse. We know we must not use deadly force to stop property theft, yet we also endorse the need to keep guns out of criminal hands. To this conundrum, there is no easy answer.

The best decision is to use the holster purse only in social or business circumstances where no other alternative exists. If unexpected circumstances put you at risk of a purse snatching, carry the holster bag cross-body, and tuck that bag in tight to the front of your body where the savvy criminal knows it is more difficult to grab. Try other holster methods, including belly bands, shoulder rigs and ankle holsters before falling back on holster bags for every day use. It is, in my opinion, a last resort.

If you decide to carry a gun in a holster handbag you must be committed to keeping that purse on your body or, if seated, between your ankles at all times. A purse hung off the back of a chair can be stolen or may attract the curiosity of a small child. Neither is acceptable when the purse contains a gun. A purse left on a host's coat tree or couch is also accessible to unauthorized hands. If you carry in a holster handbag, when you are in the car, lodge that bag tightly between the seat and console or the seat and your locked door, where it won't shift as the car moves. The gun is a serious responsibility. If you aren't willing to keep it with you continually, you must leave it safely locked away.

Clothing for Concealed Carry

A cute 25-year old student of mine complained that she couldn't carry a concealed handgun. She didn't like the feel of a fanny pack, and she had concluded an inside-the-waistband concealment holster would not fit inside the tight blue jeans she favored. The question sounded like a challenge: "Tell me how to carry my gun with no hassle, and then I'll take your advice to carry it all the time." Fortunately, there was an answer for this one: if you want to show off your rear, buy boys or men's jeans – they still fit tight in the seat, but they're roomier through the waist and will accommodate an inside-the-waistband holster and gun for most women.

A lot of armed people find themselves buying clothes to fit around concealing a gun. We select pants that have a little extra room in the waist. Our trousers have waistbands with belt loops for a sturdy belt and straight, loose legs to hide ankle holsters. We buy boxy blazers that are more loosely fitted to hide either a belt holster or shoulder holster. Others have adopted the casual photographer, hiker or mountain biker vests to hide the gun, or wear oversized shirts over tank tops in the summertime. Any jacket with an elastic band at the bottom, like bomber jackets and baseball jackets, work well for belt holster concealment, too.

It's not really as much trouble as it seems in the beginning. After a while, fitting the gun into your clothing style becomes as natural as making sure you have white underwear to wear with white slacks.

Break It In

I like to break in a holster by initially wearing it around the house so I can adjust the gear if it begins to rub or gouge. A new holster, worn immediately in public, can inflict considerable discomfort with no opportunity to make adjustments. I'd rather find out where it rubs and where it needs to be adjusted in privacy before taking it public.

A loose polo shirt covers the Para Ordnance in Jacqueline's belt holster.

I also recommend several hundred "dry" repetitions of drawing the unloaded gun from the holster, assuming a shooting stance and dry firing, when breaking in a new holster.

The body, according to physiologists, needs 2,000 to 5,000 repetitions of any movement before it becomes habit. Remember when driving a manual transmission car was nearly impossible? Now, if you drive that kind of car regularly, shifting is as automatic as tying your shoes. After around 5,000 repetitions, drawing and firing your handgun becomes just as smooth, too. You can get a good start on those repetitive movements by practicing with an unloaded gun.

Initial practice with any holster or gun must be accomplished with the weapon unloaded. Put all the ammunition in a box or drawer in a different room. Double check to see that the chamber or cylinder is empty and apply all the other principles of safe dry fire. Learning your safe way around your new holster will take some time and practice. Practice in complete privacy, without distractions or the danger of inadvertently pointing your gun at a family member.

Notes

[1] Kramer Handgun Leather, P. O. Box 112154, Tacoma, WA 98411, 253-564-6652, www.kramerleather.com

[2] Blade-Tech, 3060 S 96th, Tacoma, WA 98499, 253-581-4347, www.blade-tech.com

[3] Mitch Rosen's Extraordinary Gunleather, 300 Bedford St., Manchester, NH 03101, 603-647-2971, www.mitchrosen.com

[4] C. Rusty Sherrick, 507 Mark Dr., Elizabethtown, PA 17022, 717-361-7699, www.c-rusty.com

[5] FIST, Inc., 35 York St., Brooklyn, NY 11201, 800-443-3478 www.fist-inc.com/holsters/

[6] Matt Del Fatti, 907 W. Main St., Greenwood, WI 54437, 715-267-6420, www.delfatti.com

[7] Bianchi International, 100 Calle Cortez, Temecula, CA 92590, 800-477-8545, www.bianchi-intl.com

[8] DeSantis Holster & Leathergoods, P. O. Box 2039, Hillside Manor Branch, New Hyde Park, NY 11040, 516-354-8000, www.desantisholster.com

[9] Milt Sparks Holsters Inc., 605 E. 44th, #2, Boise, ID 82714, 208-377-5577, www.miltsparks.com

[10] Galco International, 2019 W. Quail Ave., Phoenix, AZ 85027, 602-258-8295, www.usgalco.com

[11] Five-Shot Leather, LLC, 14201 NE 36th St., Vancouver, WA 98682, 360-624-8284, www.5shotleather.com

[12] Gould & Goodrich, P. O. Box 1479, Lillington, NC 27546, 919-893-2071, www.gouldusa.com

[13] Uncle Mike's, 9200 Cody, Overland Park, KS 66214, 913-752-3400, www.unclemikes.com

[14] Coronado Leather, 120 C Ave., Coronado, CA 92118, 800-283-9509, www.coronadoleather.com.

Alessi's well-made inside-the-waistband holster (IWB) conceals beneath a conservative suit.

CHAPTER 21

The Home-Defense Shotgun

While the handgun is an easy firearm with which to learn shooting skills, it is not the most powerful defensive weapon one may choose. The handgun comes first to mind in discussion of defensive firearms because the pistol's small dimensions provide the portability and concealability valued by the individual legally entitled to carry a concealed firearm for personal defense. Other defensive functions, including home defense or protection of a place of business, may be served as well or better by a light rifle or a shotgun.

Shotguns have many great characteristics for the ensconced defender — that is, for one who must remain in position and fight instead of fleeing. The shotgun is a common home-defense and sporting firearm that not so many years ago also saw extensive use in police service. We benefit from the shotgun's long history since it provides many, many variations from which to choose, lots of ammunition options, and can fine tune the shotgun's fit with a wealth of accessories.

Terminology

With shotguns, the term "gauge" is similar to our use of "caliber" for handguns and rifles. Unlike caliber, with gauge the larger the number, the smaller the bore. Historically, gauge was defined by the number of solid balls the same diameter as the inside of the barrel that could be made from a pound of lead. Thus, the 10-gauge shotgun is larger than the 12-gauge, which is larger than the 20-gauge. Even smaller are the rather uncommon 24- and 28-gauges. The exception is the smallest of all, the .410 shotgun, which is expressed by the measurement (caliber) of its nominal bore size.

The most common shotgun gauge is the 12-gauge, the dominant shotgun choice in law enforcement. For home defense, the smaller 20-gauge shotgun does the job just fine, and this smaller shotgun is often found in use by smaller-statured birdhunters, as well.

The shotgun is unique in its ability to fire shells containing varying numbers of pellets, different sized shot, slugs, and in some guns even shells of several lengths for a magnum or standard charge. It is really quite a versatile defense tool that can be a lot of fun to train with.

The great advantage of the home-defense shotgun is its simultaneous delivery of multiple projectiles at reasonably high velocities. The effect of 20 .25-caliber pellets of #3 buckshot moving at around 1200 fps from a 20-gauge shotgun is vastly more devastating than firing nine single shots of .25 caliber handgun ammunition into an assailant. When innocent life is threatened, the overwhelming concern must be to stop the attack quickly. At that instant, we are not worried about the eventual survival or demise of the assailant; seeking only an immediate cessation of the attack. Used to stop violent attack, the shotgun is effective indeed when fired with accuracy and skill.

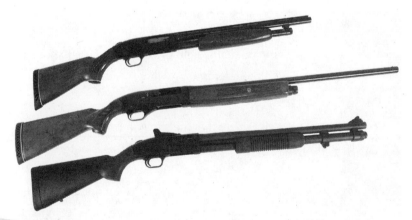

(Top to Bottom) Youth sized Mossberg Model 500 20-gauge pump shotgun, bird hunter's Winchester Model 1400 16-gauge autoloading shotgun and police-style Mossberg Model 590 12-gauge pump shotgun.

Pros and Cons

The home-defense shotgun is best employed when the home's occupants can take refuge in a prearranged, protected area, and defend themselves from a single point. The multiple projectiles that make the shotshell so effective are equally dangerous to innocents if they miss the intruder and penetrate walls of occupied rooms. Handgun ammunition poses the same danger, of course, but this hazard is compounded by the multiple projectiles each shotshell contains. Later, we'll discuss shot patterns, how they spread over varying distances, and the penetration potential of various shotgun loads.

As a defensive weapon, the shotgun seems best suited to childless couples or single occupants, or in home layouts where those to be protected are sure to be clustered behind the defender. The shotgun works well if those responsible for home defense take their position at the head of a hall that precedes all other bedrooms, or can defend the family from the top of a staircase, if all the residents are ensconced on the upper floor.

In any home-defense plan, the downfall of the shotgun will be its weight and length. If you must hold a home intruder at gun point with the shotgun for more than 10 or 15 minutes, its weight will become tiresome indeed. 12-gauge shotguns weigh around 7 lbs.; 20-g. shotguns average 5 lbs. Compare that weight to your 1- to 2-lb. handgun when deciding which home-defense tool will work best for you.

Shotgun Myths

You may have read elsewhere that the shotgun can be fired accurately without taking time to align the sights. This is not true. At home-defense distances like five yards, it is entirely possible to completely miss a human-sized target if the sights are not used! Skill with the shotgun, like any other defensive firearm, requires competent instruction, dedicated practice, sighted fire and trigger control. When these skills are mastered, it becomes a devastating weapon.

Others have written that one big disadvantage of the shotgun is that it requires two hands to operate. This is not entirely true, either. Certainly, with only one hand, it is faster and easier to fire a pistol than a shotgun. Still, with advanced training, one can operate the shotgun with just one hand, including cycling a pump shotgun.

Shotgun Selection

Just as handgun fit is crucial to accuracy, the shotgun must also fit the shooter. Women face a challenge in finding shotgun stocks that are sufficiently short. One great advantage to the 20-gauge shotgun is the ready availability of "youth models," short-stocked shotguns that operate just like the full-sized models. Most full-sized shotguns have a 14" or longer length of pull (the measurement from end of stock to trigger), while youth models usually go at 13 inches.

When the shotgun's stock is too long, the shooter's support arm is nearly hyperextended, instead of bent at the elbow for strength needed to hold up the shotgun and pull it in tightly into the shoulder. Without strong support from the non-shooting hand, the shooter leans back at the waist, attempting to balance the weight of the shotgun over her hips. If merely holding the gun was required, this would succeed;

Training to use the pump action shotgun one handed, in case of injury or disability.

After firing the first shot, brace the butt of the shotgun on the ground. The hand comes up to the forend to cycle the empty shell out of the chamber.

As the second shot fires, the recoil has opened the action slightly on this old, well-worn Remington 870.

however, when firing the shotgun, a shoulders-back stance is disastrous. When strong stance is compromised, the recoil's effects are intensified. If the overlarge shotgun is a pump action, working the slide can pull the shotgun out onto the shoulder joint, where it must be repositioned before the next shot, or it will recoil painfully into the joint.

By now, you can see the necessity of proper stock fit. As a general rule, when the butt of the shotgun is held in the elbow crook of your bent arm, the first joint crease on your index finger should fully contact the trigger. The 20-gauge youth shotguns fit this dimension perfectly for many women and should be seriously considered when buying a home-defense shotgun. If a youth model is too short, you can add a recoil pad like the Pachmayr Decelerator, which not only dampens the felt recoil enormously, but also adds length to the stock.[1]

Alternatively, the entire stock can be replaced with one with a 13" length of pull, like those sold by SPEEDFEED®[2] or the rubber overmolded 12" stock by Hogue[3]. Requiring no gunsmithing to install, replacement stocks screw onto the Remington pump or semi-auto shotguns with relative ease. A more expensive alternative is to buy a full-sized shotgun with a wood stock, then pay a gunsmith to cut the stock to size. I have done both, and swear by my short little Hogue stock.

Pump or Autoloader?

There is another variable in shotgun selection: type of action. For defensive use, we choose between semi-automatic and manually-operated shotguns (called pump shotguns). In the sporting world, double-barreled shotguns are often favored, but their ammunition capacity is too limited for defensive use. The choice between a pump and semi-automatic shotgun is similar to choosing between a semi-automatic pistol and a single-action revolver. The semi-auto shotgun employs some of the gas created by firing the shell to automatically eject the empty case and chamber fresh ammunition after each shot; the pump requires the shooter to pull the forend back to eject the empty shell, then pump it forward to recharge the chamber.

Author's favorite shotgun is an old, well-worn Remington 870 set up with good sights and a 12" length-of-pull Hogue stock that fits her perfectly.

Racking the pump gun's action to eject the empty shell and chamber another round, the shooter manually controls the supply of ammunition. On a smoothly finished pump shotgun this operation can become as automatic as shifting a manual transmission: you learn to do it almost without thinking.

The great advantage of manual operation is the gun's ability to cycle the variety of powder charges as found in different brands and kinds of ammunition. A number of semi-automatic shotguns will not cycle low-powered bird shot, an inexpensive choice students favor for training. The pump shotguns just don't care, since they need not harness the gases or the recoil-impulse generated when the shell is fired to operate the gun. A pump-action shotgun can be forced to cycle a greater variety of ammunition and can operate when dirty or unlubricated, since the shooter does all the work.

On the down side, the pump-action shotgun may produce more felt recoil than a semi-automatic shotgun of the same gauge. Most semi-automatic shotguns use the gases produced during the firing cycle, channeling gas through small holes in the barrel assembly to cycle the

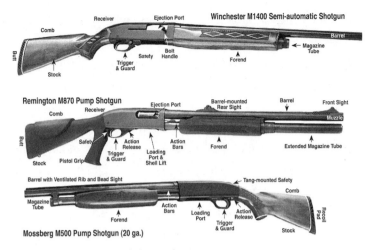

Nomenclature for common defense shotguns.

action. As a generalization, an autoloader recoils slightly less than a pump shotgun.

There are, however, two types of semi-auto shotguns, and one does not bleed off any of these gases. Typified by Benelli and Beretta brands, some semi-auto shotguns cycle the action using the recoil impulse or the energy from the rearward thrust of the burning gases. A recoil- or impulse-operated shotgun will hit just as hard as a pump shotgun.

Spending More Money

There are several modifications made by custom gunsmiths that can tame the shotgun's recoil. A barrel modification called backboring reduces felt recoil by redistributing the gases created by the burning powder, and as a side benefit it rearranges the pellets into a tighter shot group that does not spread as widely in flight to the target. Best in the business for this after-market modification is Hans Vang, who developed the Vang Comp System[4] and has worked his magic on both my "working" and competition shotguns.

Major modifications aside, a competent gunsmith can do much to simply "slick up" the operation of your shotgun. On the pump gun, this means smoothing away any rough places on the action bars and related working parts. Some of the same effect can be accomplished by pumping the action thousands of times, which could be accomplished practicing dry fire.

Extensive dry fire isn't recommended for shotguns, however, as it is feared that the long firing pin may crack from vibrations that run through the metal during dry fire. If your manual shotgun cycles roughly, however, you can do everything but pull the trigger, racking the action repeatedly until the parts wear themselves into a smoother fit. The action release lever will have to be used if the trigger is not pulled; otherwise the action will remain locked closed.

Another common after-market modification is shotgun sights. Many shotguns come from the factory with no rear sight whatsoever, just one or two beads on a ventilated rib running along the top of many sporting shotguns. Slug guns, set up for deer hunting, are the common exception, wearing better buckhorn or pistol style sights but their rifled barrels don't work for bird shot or buck shot, since the rifling slings the shot toward the edges of a large circle with no shot in the center.

I believe a self-defense shotgun absolutely requires a good set of sights. Variations include a rear notch and front blade that are very like pistol sights; or a ghost ring rear sight that is much like an aperture sight, commonly used with a blade front sight. In my opinion, the Express Sight designed by Ashley Emerson and marketed by XS Sights[5] can't be beat on the shotgun. The latter three are excellent choices for the combat shotgun, although the beads will suffice for those who will simply pursue basic competence with their home-defense shotgun at relatively short distances.

Your skill with your defensive shotgun will be only as good as the practice and training time you put in with your equipment. Good technique is the first step in rendering the shotgun enjoyable for training and informal practice. The second step is setting up the shotgun so it is comfortable. Let's outline some of the accessories that make a difference.

Before you set out to replace the recoil pad on your shotgun, look at your undies. Metal parts on brassiere straps are downright dangerous

Ghost ring shotgun sights

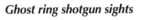
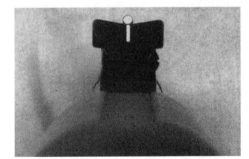

XS Sight's express sight system

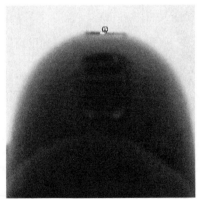

The simple bead sight, illustrated in the first photo somewhat elevated, and in the second in the position used to aim the shotgun.

beneath the butt of a recoiling shotgun! My favorite cure is the PAST Hidden Comfort Recoil Shield[6] for women, which is secured beneath the bra strap with several Velcro strips. Another cure is to wear a sports bra without any metal, but that won't offer any recoil protection.

If the recoil really bothers you, consider having a gunsmith fit a Pachmayr Decelerator butt pad on the end of your shotgun. This incredible accessory absorbs and distributes the recoil like nobody's business–it is well worth the price!

Technique Eases the Pain

Listen up, this is important: firing the shotgun doesn't have to hurt! Let's look at why people get bruised shooting the shotgun and see if we can prevent bad first experiences, as well as offer techniques that will make shooting more pleasant.

Just like the pistol, there is a proper grip for the shotgun. Because of the shotgun's weight, we have a tendency to encircle the stock with the shooting hand thumb, a habit I fight to this day. That would work, if just holding up the gun was required. Unfortunately, when the shotgun moves back under recoil, a "wrapped" thumb can strike the nose with considerable force.

RULE #1: TO AVOID NOSEBLEEDS ON THE SHOTGUN RANGE, POINT THE SHOOTING-HAND THUMB TOWARD THE MUZZLE.

Other dangers to avoid are too-long fingernails. I have seen the nails of the shooting hand gouge the cheek when the shooting hand and face come too close during recoil. Nose bleeds and cheek gouges don't happen to everyone: variables include the length of the stock and where the shooter cheeks the comb.

Find the Shoulder Pocket

Improper placement of the shotgun on the shoulder joint is the leading cause of shooting discomfort with the self-defense shotgun. Many folks learned to shoot a rifle as the first gun they ever fired, and they attempt to apply the traditional rifle marksman's stance to the shotgun. Unlike a rifle, the defensive shotgun will be fired with heavily recoiling buckshot and slugs. If fired with the butt against the shoulder joint, the collar bone or lower, on breast tissue, it will hurt!

To locate the proper spot for the shotgun butt, try the following exercise that I learned at Clint Smith's Thunder Ranch:[7] Put your fingers in your shooting-side armpit; flatten your hand, and let the thumb point up. The area the thumb touches (between the armpit and center of your chest) is called the shoulder pocket. Raise and lower the shooting-side elbow, and feel the musculature beneath your thumb move up and down the chest. If the butt of the shotgun is placed where your thumb touches, those muscles help protect against bruising.

It is my experience that squaring your shoulders to face the target is the best protection against the shotgun slipping out onto the shoulder joint during multiple shots. A bladed stance invites the shotgun to slip out of the shoulder pocket.

RULE #2: FIND THE SHOULDER POCKET, AND PULL THE BUTT OF THE SHOTGUN AGAINST IT FIRMLY. This rearward pull is exerted with the strong hand, which also operates the safety and the trigger. Do not discharge the shotgun unless it is pressed tightly into the shoulder pocket, with the torso squared to the target!

Although counterintuitive, the straight thumb of the shooting hand is the key to avoiding socking your own nose during recoil.

X marks the spot! The shoulder pocket is magic for avoiding bruising and pain from shotgun recoil.

Jacqueline takes care to get the butt of the shotgun in the shoulder pocket before shooting.

Many shotgun trainers teach that raising the shooting-side elbow enhances the protection of the shoulder pocket. Some circumstances do not permit the raised elbow, however, including extending the elbow beyond cover or concealment. I favor a lower elbow position, for more strength with which to pull the stock into my shoulder. You can choose what works best for you.

Why is it so important to press the butt of the shotgun tightly in the shoulder pocket? The shotgun's recoil is considerable. When the shotgun is pressed tightly against the shooter's chest, the jolt of the recoil is like receiving a hard push. It rolls you back, but does not injure. If the recoiling shotgun is held loosely or is actually slightly away from the shoulder, it comes back with brutal impact, and is like taking a full power, fisted punch. Which would you prefer?

Body Position

We are limited in our efforts to eliminate recoil in the defensive shotgun, yet the power of the weapon is both its strength and disadvantage. Proper grip and shoulder position mitigate most of the discomfort, yet the shooter must still contend with the rearward thrust, which can throw a slightly built person off balance unless body dynamics and strength are harnessed to tip the equation in our favor.

If the shotgun shooter's legs are locked and rigid, the recoil pushes the shooter back off balance, moved rearward all the way to their toes. On the other hand, if the knees are bent, the legs act as shock absorbers, allowing the shooter to flex with the recoil, then spring immediately forward to regain the shooting stance.

I prefer a deep bend in the forward, non-shooting side knee, with less in the rear, shooting-side leg. The deep flex of the forward knee

Unlike classic riflery, the shotgunning stance positions hips and shoulders square to the target.

brings the shoulders well forward of the hips, and puts the hips forward of the rear knee and foot. The aggressive, forward-leaning posture puts all the weight of the body behind the recoiling shotgun, and uses that weight to bring the muzzle down and reassume a shooting position for follow-up shots.

Which brings us to *RULE #3: LEAN AGGRESSIVELY INTO THE SHOTGUN TO ENJOY RECOIL CONTROL AND MAINTAIN BALANCE.*

The final element of body positioning for successful, pain-free shotgun shooting is the placement of the cheek on the comb of the stock. Firm pressure between cheek and stock is essential. If the cheek is slightly off the stock, the blow can be debilitating when the shotgun recoils and socks its operator in the jaw. Just as the stock is pulled tightly into the shoulder pocket, a firm cheek "weld" is an important way to avoid shooting pain.

An excellent after-market product for both carbines and shotguns encourages a consistent cheek weld, while reducing the amount of recoil felt on the cheek and jaw. An adhesive-backed pad, made of rubbery Sorbothane® is marketed as the Cheek-eez pad through the Brownells catalog.[8]

RULE #4: PRESS YOUR CHEEK FIRMLY TO THE STOCK, CONTACTING THE COMB IN THE SAME PLACE EVERY TIME. There is a secondary advantage to developing a cheek weld that is repeatable every time the shotgun comes to your shoulder. If you cheek the comb the same place every time, your use of the shotgun sights will be consistent and once the proper position is memorized, the cheek weld is the key to quick sight acquisition.

As we discussed earlier, the most common shotgun sights are a single bead, double beads, ghost-ring sights or rifle-style sights. When you cheek the stock, the sight alignment should be similar to the earlier illustrations. If the sights are out of alignment when you bring the shotgun up on target, experiment with cheeking the stock on a different part of your face. Where the cheek contacts the comb will vary from individual to individual, depending on face shape, length of neck, and

Strong shotgunning stance counteracts the recoil's rearward push, seen here, and allows small shooter to maintain balance and control for multiple shots with the 12-gauge.

how well the shotgun fits the individual. I press the comb of the stock right below my upper mandible, while others contact the stock at the jaw line. The more sophisticated sporting shotgun shooters fine-tune cheeking the stock by changing the drop of the shotgun stock's comb, but combat shotgunners usually just learn to work with a straight field stock.

Operating the Combat Shotgun

Loading a shotgun is much more of a manual one-at-a-time affair than using a magazine or speed loader to load a semi-auto pistol or revolver. Odd, tubular speedloaders exist for shotguns, but are primarily used by competitive shooters and are extremely specialized. The defensive shotgunner may increase ammunition capacity by installing an extended magazine tube, but beyond that, we simply make best use of the ammunition we have and are prepared to transition to handgun if we shoot the shotgun "dry."

Non-emergency loading of the shotgun consists of filling only the magazine tube. Most shotguns in common use do not have internal firing pin blocks, so are at risk of accidentally discharging if they fall or are dropped with a shell in the chamber. Indeed, internal drop safeties, which are standard on later model Mossberg shotguns are the exception, not the rule.

This is why we do not leave the home-defense shotgun sitting in a corner or on a shelf with a loaded chamber. If the danger of home invasion is so great that there is no time to chamber a round, a firearm will not solve the problem. Good locks, solid doors and windows, and other precautions should address that danger.

Unlike the procedure for handguns, loading the shotgun is a relatively slow and dexterity-intensive job. The shotgun's "magazine" is a tube beneath the barrel, nearly always accessed through the bottom of the receiver, into which we feed the shot shells one at a time. On most shotguns, the action must be closed before the magazine can be loaded. Unmodified shotguns usually accept four rounds, although as noted earlier an extension to the tube may accommodate seven or eight shells. If the tube accepts only one or two shells, take it off and check for a magazine block, commonly installed to make the gun legal for bird hunting.

To simplify loading, Louis Awerbuck teaches his students to "trace" the final half-inch of the trigger guard with the tip of the shell, guiding it into the magazine tube. On shotguns like the common Remington 1100/11-87s this brings the front of the cartridge in contact with the carrier release, which must be depressed to open the loading port. On other shotguns, his method gives an index to guide the shell into the loading port, even in the dark. Awerbuck gained recognition teaching at Gunsite in its heyday, then began his own instructional firm, Yavapai Firearms Academy.[9] He travels to locations throughout the U.S. and his training is well worth the tuition. He is also author of the authoritative textbook *The Defensive Shotgun: Techniques & Tactics* published by Delta Press.[10]

Once the shell is inside the loading port, use your thumb to push on its base until it is in the magazine tube completely. Pushing against the pressure of the magazine spring, you'll feel the cartridge catch

Hans Vang makes and sells this magazine extension tube for 12-gauge shotguns.

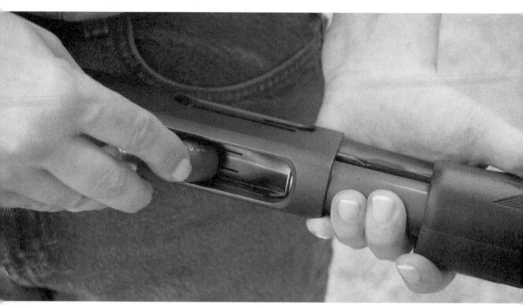

The slow process of feeding one shell at a time to the shotgun's magazine tube.

when it goes past the shell stops. Configured slightly differently on various shotguns, the shell stops are small metal claws on either side of the mouth of the magazine tube that keep the shells inside the tube despite the pressure of the magazine spring. Take a look now at your unloaded shotgun and find the shell stops; we'll revisit them later.

If the shotgun is brought into action, you will need to chamber a shell. Cycle the shotgun's action to move a shot shell from the magazine tube, onto the shell carrier and up into the chamber. With the pump gun, that will mean depressing the action release and pulling the forend all the way back to put a shell on the carrier, then pushing it forward so the shell is lifted into the chamber and the action closed.

On most semi-automatics, pull back the operating handle until the action locks open. This brings a shell out of the tube, and if you look in, you can see it sitting on the carrier before the action closes, chambering the shot shell. Benellis and Berettas use a different sequence, due to their tactical advantage of being able to leave a shell on the carrier with the action closed. Hitting a small button mounted on the side of the receiver puts a shell on the shell lift where it can sit indefinitely until the shooter racks the action to load the chamber.

Unloading Professionally

Now its time to discuss proper unloading. "Can't I just pump the shells out of my shotgun to unload?" a student always asks during our defensive shotgun classes. You can, but there is a better way that first empties the chamber, then keeps it empty for maximum safety.

First, remove the round from the chamber. Engage the safety and open the action, being careful to maintain safe muzzle direction. The chamber round should eject; you can catch it if you open the action slowly. With most shotguns, this step will have positioned a shell on the carrier or shell lifter. Roll the shotgun over, so the ejection port faces down. The shell on the carrier should fall into your hand. Carefully check by sight and feel to ascertain that the chamber is indeed empty.

Watching carefully to assure the chamber remains empty, close the action. The chamber should remain empty as you close the action, because you have removed the shell from the carrier. On most shotguns, a new shell shouldn't feed from the magazine tube without fully cycling the action. Turn the gun over, so you look down into the loading port. With the tip of your finger, depress the shell stop.

Be sure each shotgun shell you load goes well past the shell stops, so you don't create your own malfunction.

The shell may remain in place, constrained by the shell stop on the opposite side. Use your thumb to wiggle the shell free. When it pops past the shell stops, lift it from the loading port and repeat the process until all the shot shells are out of the magazine tube.

Before declaring the shotgun unloaded, open the action again and double check both the chamber and magazine tube visually. Insert your finger into the empty chamber for a manual inspection. Reach lower and feel for the magazine follower to be sure a shell is not present. If the gun is simply being stored, the magazine tube should be empty so the compressed metal spring does not take a "set."

Don't be discouraged if this unloading process is difficult at first. The thumb and fingers may seem too big for the limited space inside the loading port, yet it feels like you need three hands to get the job done! Persevere, and you will learn how to jimmy the shell stops, carrier and shell into position where the shell pops out easily.

Learning how to properly unload your shotgun is important. It keeps you from having to chamber and manually eject each round when you need to unload the shotgun, reducing wear and damage to the shells. Safety must come first, over any perceived inconvenience! Pumping the shells out of the magazine tube is the mark of an amateur.

Tactics for the Home-Defense Shotgun

As discussed in the previous chapter, the shotgun is an excellent survival tool for the defender ensconced in a safe room, prepared to defend self and family if the intruder ignores warnings and breaks through the door. This scenario presumes that the defender knows the direction in which the shotgun pellets will travel and is certain no innocents are in the path of the shot. The shotgun is best applied to home layouts where children's rooms lie behind the defender. In home layouts where rooms are scattered throughout the home, young children will need to be quietly evacuated to the safe area as quickly as is safely practical. If, within the constraints of your circumstances, this does not seem possible, the shotgun may not be your best choice.

In apartments, safe rooms must be arranged so the area into which the pellets will fly is backed by bullet-stopping material, something scarce in urban housing. While nothing short of heavy concrete or masonry construction gives full bullet-stopping ability, careful shot placement into known uninhabited directions is necessary for those who plan to use the shotgun's multiple pellets in home defense.

The shotgun is not the best weapon to take prowling through your house to check out a noise in the night. Not only are house searches dangerous, the long muzzle of the shotgun may alert a waiting intruder to your approach, so he may grab and lever it from your hands. The shotgun's size makes it more difficult to move quietly, avoiding furniture, lamps and other household objects. Return to lesson one: don't search your house if you believe you have an intruder in the home! Call the police and let them do it!

Weapon retention techniques have been developed for the shotgun; if you adopt this weapon you owe it to yourself and your loved ones to get the proper training in its use and retention. Know how to accurately shoot your shotgun, and know how to keep it in your hands if the assailant tries to take it from you. One advantage of the "Arm Tuck" shooting stance taught by author Massad Ayoob and defined in his shotgun book *StressFire II: Advanced Defensive Shotgun*[11] is the ability to withdraw the muzzle somewhat while remaining in a firing stance. It is also a good fall back stance for shooters who do not wish to take the impact of the recoil on the shoulder, and when the shotgun is grossly oversized for the shooter. It is only good for targets at relatively close range.

The shotgun, handgun or rifle each has defensive advantages and tactical disadvantages. Serious self- and home-defense practitioners often pursue proficiency with more than one defensive weapon system available, to increase the chances that they and their family can survive criminal attack. In trained hands, the shotgun is a most formidable self defense tool.

In Ayoob's "Arm Tuck" shotgunning stance, the comb of this big Browning Auto 5 shotgun is pressed firmly into both the front and rear tendons of the armpit. The barrel is seen in the low peripheral vision and can thus be roughly aimed. Ayoob learned this technque from the late Bill Groce when he was head of firearms training for Ohio Peace Officers Training Academy.

Notes

[1] Pachmayr, 800-423-9704, www.lymanproducts.com/pachmayr/.

[2] SPEEDFEED®, 13386 International Parkway, Jacksonville, FL 32218 800-433-2909 www.speedfeedinc.com.

[3] Hogue Inc., P. O. Box 1138, Paso Robles, CA 93447 800-438-4747, ww.hogueinc.com.

[4] Vang Comp Systems, 400 W. Butterfield Rd., Chino Valley, AZ 86323 928-636-8455 www.vangcomp.com.

[5] XS Sight Systems, 2401 Ludelle St., Ft. Worth, TX 76105 888-744-4880, www.xssights.com.

[6] PAST Hidden Comfort Shield, Battenfield Technologies, 5885 W Van Horn Tavern Rd., Columbia, MO 65203 573-446-3857 http://www.battenfeldtechnologies.com/360000.html

[7] Training resources quoted: Thunder Ranch, op. cit.; Lethal Force Institute, op. cit.; http://www.Yavapai Firearms Academy, P. O. Box 27290, Prescott Valley, AZ 86312 928-772-8262, yfainc.com.

[8] Brownells, op. cit.

[9] Yavapai Firearms Academy, op. cit.

[10] Delta Press, 215 S. Washington Ave., El Dorado, AR 71730 870-8626-3811 www.deltapress.com

[11] Police Bookshelf, op. cit.

CHAPTER 22

Shotgun Ammunition

S hotgun ammunition choices range from slugs to buckshot to small game loads and birdshot. To give you an idea of the differences within just one category, Federal Cartridge Company sells a half dozen different slugs (a solid, single projectile) in weights ranging from the 1-3/4 oz. 10-gauge slug; 1-1/4- or 1-oz. slugs for the 12-gauge; a 4/5-oz. slug for the 16-gauge; the common 3/4-oz. slug for the 20-gauge; and finally a 1/4-oz. slug for the .410-caliber shotgun.

The list is several times longer for buckshot, since it comes in at least seven different sizes of shot, and may be loaded in either 3" "Magnum" shells or 2-3/4" "Maximum" shells for 12-gauge, 16-gauge or 20-gauge shotguns. (Note that the length of the shotgun shell refers to its "opened-up" length after it has been fired.) On the topic of birdshot and field loads, the choices are as numerous as the different gauges multiplied by ten or more sizes of shot and BBs used to hunt everything from tiny doves to large geese.

Out of all the choices in shotgun ammunition, we need to study two categories for home defense: buckshot and slugs. Some will advise you to load your home-defense shotgun with bird shot "because it won't go through the walls." That statement is incorrect, false and dead wrong! We have fired birdshot through three layers of half-inch sheet rock. Whether it would penetrate the body cavity after going through walls is questionable, yet there remains potential for harm to delicate tissue like eyes.

However, that is not my argument against such advice. Even without intervening obstacles like walls, bodily penetration by field, game, or bird shot is too shallow to reach vital organs on an adult-

#8 Birdshot

#4 Birdshot is larger and heavier than #8.

Buckshot made for the 20-ga. (abbreviation for "gauge") shotgun

#4 buckshot is the smallest buckshot for the 12-ga. shotgun.

#1 Buckshot for 12-ga. shotgun.

Pronounced "single aught," #0 buckshot in a 12-ga. shell.

#00 ("double-aught") buckshot is the most common buckshot for 12-ga. shotguns.

The monstrous .36-caliber pellets of the 12-ga. #000 ("triple-aught") buckshot shell.

20-ga. shotgun slug.

A 12-ga. Foster-style shot-gun slug.

A sabot slug is a more aerodynamic projectile housed inside the plastic sabot during its trip down the shotgun barrel. Once past the muzzle, the sabot falls away.

sized assailant, a problem compounded by thick clothing, obesity or heavy musculature. In bare ballistic gelatin, birdshot will penetrate just six to eight inches, but placing multiple layers of fabric on the face of the gelatin block seriously impairs performance. By comparison, #00 buckshot can penetrate up to 16 inches on bare gelatin and manages to penetrate 10-12 inches beyond simulated clothing.

The larger the projectile, the deeper the penetration. This is certainly the case with the next kind of shotgun ammunition we'll discuss: slugs. The 1-oz. 12-gauge shotgun slug is capable of devastating stopping power. Some folks, including Marty Hayes, director of The Firearms Academy of Seattle[1], have gone so far as to recommend loading only slugs in the 20-gauge shotgun, bypassing buckshot altogether. Personally, I would temper that advice, commenting that the slug is simply designed to do a different job than buckshot.

Slugs best serve the shotgunner's long distance and extreme accuracy shooting needs. With decent sights, a skilled operator can hit accurately with a slug out to 100 yards, farther than we might anticipate using the gun in home defense, yet a very real necessity for law enforcement officers or for hunters. Slugs can also penetrate glass, wood and automobiles, needs also more common to law enforcement duties.

Buckshot Choices

With buckshot, penetration is influenced by size and velocity of the projectiles, more than the gauge of shotgun from which it is fired. Larger buckshot is recommended where heavy clothing or intervening obstacles may interfere with penetration. Where it would be difficult to anticipate an obese or leather-clad assailant, the differences between summer and winter weather in many areas can certainly indicate light or heavy clothing.

Because body mass is also impossible to predict, it might be more sensible to load the home-defense shotgun with a medium-sized buckshot like the common 20 gauge #3 buckshot, or #1 buckshot in the 12-gauge. While penetration is not likely to be as deep as with the more common #00 buckshot, the slightly smaller shot simultaneously introduces a lot of projectiles, creating a devastating wound channel.

The following chart lists common buck shot sizes, with the largest shot shown first. To help you compare, the size of the shot is described here in caliber, which you will remember from handgunning is the measurement of the projectile at its greatest diameter.

Shot Size	ShotshellCaliber	Qty in Shell	# Pellets
000 buckshot	3" Magnum 12-ga.	.36 caliber	10
00 buckshot*	2-3/4" Maximum 12-ga.	.33 caliber	9-12
0 buckshot	2-3/4" Maximum 12-ga.	.32 caliber	12
#1 buckshot	2-3/4" Maximum 12-ga.	.30 caliber	16
#2 buckshot	3" Magnum 20-ga.	.27 caliber	18
#3 buckshot	2-3/4" Maximum 20-ga.	.25 caliber	20
#4 buckshot **	2-3/4" Maximum 12-ga.	.24 caliber	27

* With 00 buckshot, 3" Magnum shells contain 15 pellets; 2-3/4" Magnum shells contain 12 pellets, and the low-recoil law enforcement loads have just nine.

** With #4 buckshot, 3" Magnum shells contain 41 pellets; 2-3/4" Magnum shells contain 34 pellets. The magnum shells recoil viciously, in my opinion, and are to be avoided.

In choosing buckshot, you will sometimes face additional choices. For example, #4 buckshot is sold in Magnum 3" shotshells containing 41 pellets, 2-3/4" Magnum shells with 34 pellets, and 2-3/4" Maximum shot shells with just 27 pellets. The last 27-pellet shell will recoil less than the Magnum cartridges, which must push the heavier payload of more pellets. And, if you've chosen the 20-gauge, the #3 buckshot recoils considerably less than #00 buckshot from a 12-gauge.

Shot Spread

Until we understand how buckshot behaves after it exits the shotgun's barrel, the idea of simultaneously unleashing from nine to 27 pellets seems pretty risky. Testing your own shotgun is the key to knowing where and how it will hit with different brands and sizes of buckshot. The distribution of the shot pellets striking the target is called "patterning." Every shotgun will pattern differently, and the same shotgun will pattern differently with different ammunition. Only hands-on experience at the range will show you what to expect from your own shotgun and the ammunition you have chosen.

Expect the buckshot pattern to expand at approximately one inch per yard between the muzzle and the target with 12-gauge #00 buckshot. The pattern will be larger with 20-gauge #3 buckshot and with 12 gauge #4 buckshot. That means that shot fired across a seven-yard-wide bedroom should cluster in a six- to eight-inch circle, depending on ammunition and the shotgun. Additional factors affect how tightly the shot patterns. The first is the ammunition; the second is the addition of a choke tube, which can be used to constrict that column of shot as it leaves the shotgun barrel. Another method to tighten shot groups is backboring, which lengthens the forcing cone and changes how the shot travels down the barrel. Hans Vang of Vang Comp Systems[2] is the leading source of this defensive shotgun modification.

Since we're addressing ammunition, let's discuss how the shot itself affects the size of the pattern. Shot may be either copper-plated or bare

#4 buckshot fired 10 yards from target using 12-ga. shotgun.

#1 buckshot fired 10 yards from the target using 16-ga. shotgun.

#00 Buckshot fired 10 yards from target using 12-ga. shotgun; two slugs in head of target.

#3 buckshot fired from 10 yards with 20-ga. shotgun; two 20-ga. slugs in head of target.

lead. The harder copper-plated shot reduces denting that can occur while the shot is being propelled down the barrel. A dented pellet that is no longer spherical will fly erratically, expanding an otherwise good shot pattern. (Steel shot is also sold, but as it is commonly used in game loads, not buckshot, it doesn't really play a part in home defense.)

Confused?

While much of the foregoing is perhaps more detailed than you need, I've included it to give you an overview of shotgun ammunition. At the risk of oversimplification, I believe it boils down to home defense choices of a 20-gauge or 12-gauge shotgun, as indicated by your strength, stature and how much recoil you can control. For home defense, I would load the shotgun's magazine tube with buckshot, and keep some slugs readily at hand for unexpected circumstances requiring very fine accuracy.

The 16-gauge shotgun would also make a fine home-defense weapon, but the owner may have trouble finding a readily available variety of ammunition, especially at budget prices like those that come along at large chain stores and gun shows. And, like any other defense weapon, the shotgun is only as effective as the shooter's training, practice and confidence, and those come only from training and regular practice.

Notes

[1] The Firearms Academy of Seattle, Inc., P. O. Box 400, Onalaska, WA 98570 www.firearmsacademy.com 360-978-6100

[2] Vang Comp, op cit.

CHAPTER 23

Rifles and Carbines

I s there any place for the light rifle or carbine (a carbine is simply a short-barreled rifle) in the private citizen's self-defense arsenal, or is it best carried by cops, sheriffs and soldiers? I asked instructors John and Vicki Farnam, who responded with a story:

A woman and her children were in their remote Montana home when a warning came over the radio that authorities believed an escaped, dangerous prisoner was in their area. The announcement put the woman in a heightened state of awareness, so she was prepared when some while later she spotted a lone figure walking up her mile-and-a-half driveway.

Standing on her porch, rifle in hand, she ordered the stranger to come no closer. When he ignored repeated verbal warnings and continued to approach, the woman shot him in one knee. With determined aggression, the man continued to approach the home. Her second shot took out his other knee. The woman held him at gunpoint for law enforcement officers, who confirmed her fear that she had indeed encountered the escapee.

The rifle extended this woman's perimeter of safety dramatically. The escapee's proximity would have endangered the family if he had approached to within the distances most handgunners would confidently make a shot on a moving aggressor. The tactics of this situation underscore the very real danger of being overrun by the aggressor and sometimes their accomplices, as well. People who are shot with a handgun can remain aggressive and assaultive for some time before the wound incapacitates them. In this dangerous time gap, the home defender can be killed or seriously injured if the invader is too close. The rifle extends the effective marksmanship range to prevent this danger.

At the same time, we can legally and ethically shoot only a person we have clearly identified as a deadly danger to ourselves or other innocents. The rifle's ability to control distance must be balanced by the home owner's clear-headed analysis of the situation.

"We're hearing the term 'urban rifle' to describe a rifle used for defense between 30 and 150 meters," John Farnam elaborates. These distances allow target identification and verbal warnings, both vital elements of legally justifiable self defense. And at any distance, if circumstances allow all-out escape, it is heartily recommended.

As you know from the following chapter, I am an enthusiastic advocate of the personal defense shotgun. Still, most shotguns are effective only out to 12 to 14 yards with buckshot, unless the shooter has a safe backstop behind the assailant that she knows will absorb a buckshot pattern that has spread beyond the size of the assailant's body. A slug can certainly be substituted in such circumstances, but unless they have shot the weapon extensively with slugs, shotgun-armed home defenders may lack confidence in their marksmanship, especially at longer distances. Because the recoil discomfits them, few shooters practice enough to realize long-range competence with their shotgun loaded with slugs.

A rudimentary rifle or carbine is unhampered by the problem of shot spread, and smaller calibers are almost free of recoil. Over and over, we see beginners' faces light up after firing their first shot through a .223 carbine. The comparatively light recoil of the rifle or carbine has another advantage: that of nearly instant recoil recovery and the ability to accurately deliver rapid, multiple shots. For this task, it will be hard to surpass the .223 Remington caliber (the civilian equivalent of the military's 5.56mm NATO cartridge). This caliber will generally show muzzle velocities of 3,000 feet per second for the common 55-grain bullet.

Rifle ammunition generally derives its power not from the weight

Federal legislation restricting features available on the AR-15 style rifle has run up the cost in recent years, until what was once an affordable home-defense tool has become a major equipment investment.

The Ruger Ranch Rifle (Mini-14) is a .223 caliber rifle that has none of the militaristic appearance that seems to alarm legislators and antigun activists.

In 2008 Ruger redressed their classic Mini-14 in a rubber overmold Hogue stock, with a blued finish, and a handy 16-1/8" barrel and dubbed it the NRA Mini-14. With each one sold, Ruger makes a contribution to the NRA Institute for Legislative Action to support our gun rights.

of the projectile, but from its high velocity. Even so, an assailant may be hit with a .223 rifle bullet without immediate incapacitation. The harder-recoiling .308 Winchester rifle cartridge is capable of a more decisive result, but its compromises eliminate some of the advantages of a defensive carbine.

Overpenetration of larger caliber rifle bullets must be considered. Most hunting rounds are capable of penetrating wall after wall of modern housing construction. This very real hazard makes selection of ammunition that will not overpenetrate exceedingly crucial with any rifle, even a .223. In the book *Ultimate Sniper*[1] author John Plaster reports that a .308 bullet that has gone through a body still maintains the power of a .357 Magnum handgun bullet, although it has lost half of its velocity. These concerns should raise a very serious warning to those considering a rifle for home defense in a multi-person household, apartment building or densely populated area. Remember, even if your reason for discharging a firearm is completely justified, you remain responsible for harm inflicted beyond your immediate threat.

Further, fewer semi-automatic rifles are chambered for the larger .308 caliber, and tend to be considerably more expensive than the .223 carbine. The .308 rifle will be heavier than most .223s. Finally, the concussion of firing a .308 inside a confined space is vastly more disorienting and deafening than doing so with a .223, which is certainly bad enough. For the same reasons, other hunting rifle calibers like the .30-30, .30-06 or 7mm Magnum are not suitable for home defense.

So Many Rifles

Semi-automatic rifles that work well for ensconced defense scenarios include the ubiquitous "black rifles," derived from Eugene Stoner's original AR-15 design. Although Colt's Manufacturing was long the primary source of AR-15s, nowadays Remington, Rock River Arms, Olympic Arms, Bushmaster, DPMS, Armalite, Sabre Defence and others have divided the market share.

The prevalence of state and federal gun restriction laws has put the price and availability of the AR-15 and its clones out of reach for some shooters. A very serviceable alternative is the semi-automatic Ruger Mini-14 or Ruger Ranch Rifle chambered in .223 Rem. It is not too heavy and is short stocked for a good fit for small-statured shooters right out of the box.

The Ruger Ranch Rifle, the civilian version of the Mini-14, is drilled and tapped for scope rings, so installing optical sights is easily accomplished, depending on the use envisioned. For home-defense distances, the rifle's rudimentary peep sight should serve just fine. If you begin to enjoy practice and casual competition with your Ruger, the sights may be the first feature you wish to upgrade, possibly with a telescopic sight, commonly called a scope.

Author and Massad Ayoob test-drive the Sabre Defence AR-15 rifles wearing the "Massad Ayoob Signature Series" imprimatur.

Both the Ranch Rifle and AR-15s are magazine fed. The magazines make reloading or switching to specialty ammunition for different degrees of penetration a quick, relatively simple task, which is not true of other rifle operating systems.

Radical Caliber Change

An alternative "urban" rifle is a carbine chambered for a pistol cartridge. "Some people argue that a carbine is just a big, clumsy handgun," John Farnam contends, "but that's not true." He noted that the pistol-caliber carbine has a considerably longer sight radius than a pistol, that most handgun bullets develop much higher velocities in the long barrel and that these guns generally have sights far superior to the handgun.

The pistol-caliber carbine recoils considerably less than a handgun firing the same cartridge and is relatively quiet when discharged. These features make them very pleasant firearms with which to practice and simply enjoy recreational marksmanship. Farnam reported that he has seen women shoot hundreds of rounds comfortably with such carbines, becoming deadly accurate in the process. Excellent "companion" guns to the handgun, they allow the owner to keep one caliber of ammunition on hand for use in both weapons.

The carbine offers good accuracy out to 100 meters, for threat management where an assailant has been clearly identified and has disobeyed warnings to leave. Beretta's CX4 Storm, chambered for 9mm or .45 ACP pistol cartridges, carries on a tradition formerly exemplified by the Marlin Camp Carbine and Ruger's PC carbine, both now discontinued.

Another pistol caliber carbine that deserves thoughtful consideration for home defense is the manually operated lever action. While we think of this firearm as the province of those fun-loving cowboy action shooters, it has the potential to serve the serious duty of defense, too.

Common calibers include .38 Special, .357 Magnum, .44 Special and .44 Magnum, with cartridges generally loaded in a magazine tube banded beneath the barrel. A round is chambered by working the lever, although due to the nature of many of these gun's safety mechanism (most only have a cross bolt safety), I would do with the lever-action carbine as I do with a shotgun: store it chamber-empty until ready to use, unless the manufacturer specifically describes internal safety provisions to avoid an inertia discharge.

On initial consideration, it might seem that a manually operated gun like a lever-action carbine may be too slow for self defense, although that cycle differs little from the pump shotgun. With practice and habituation, the manual cycle to remove the empty shell and replace it with fresh ammunition can become smooth, natural and quick. The reload will be slower, because only one cartridge at a time can be loaded into the magazine tube, introduced through a tiny loading port.

Pistol caliber carbines are not as popular as more modern rifles, because despite their rifle-like size, the ballistic performance of these guns will never approach that of a .223 or .308. However, I believe they deserve serious consideration for home defense for their user-friendly operating systems, handgun ammunition compatibility, easy aiming qualities, milder noise and recoil when discharged, and the tendency for hollowpoint pistol ammunition to stop inside the assailant's body.

Sighting Issues

Probably the most common rifle accessory is an optical or telescopic sighting device. Because rifles have seen more traditional service in hunting and competitive sports, a telescopic sight or "scope" has been the common method to increase ability to see and aim at distances of 100, 300, 500 yards or more. Defensive rifle uses generally occur within the 10- to 50-yard range, and 100 yards represents an extreme distance for justifiable defense by a private citizen. In this venue, traditional hunting-type scopes represent more disadvantage than benefit.

Fixed iron sights, while preferred for home defense, also present their own challenge. The greatest one is learning and remembering that the rifle, designed for more distant targets may not hit the exact spot covered by the iron sights at closer distances. This is a concern for the AR-15 rifle system, on which the rear sight is mounted on top of the carrying handle several inches above the barrel, creating a "mechanical offset" that is comparable to parallax between the viewfinder and lens of a camera. A close-range shot with an AR-15 will strike several inches below the point covered by the front sight.

Competent training and serious practice allow the rifle owner to commit these disparities to memory, and if a precise shot is required at close distances the shooter compensates for the mechanical offset by holding the sights an inch or two higher than the spot they wish to strike. If these possibilities seem obscure, let me admit that more than one police officer has put a crease across the hood of a patrol car behind which they took cover before shooting. The mechanical offset of their AR-15's sights gave a clear sight picture, but the barrel itself was obstructed by the car body, a difference forgotten in the heat of an emergency.

If discussing home defense, it is difficult to imagine any viable threat beyond 50 yards, unless the carbine's role includes "protecting" a garden, livestock and pets. While it is common to sight in, or "zero," a rifle or carbine to hit precisely at a 100- or even 200-yard distance, it may be more reasonable for the home-defense rifle owner to sight her gun in for 50 yard targets. Even then, a rudimentary understanding of bullet trajectory, mechanical offset and such factors is necessary.

Upon leaving the rifle's barrel, the bullet begins a slightly upward path of travel, called its trajectory. After the bullet reaches the apex of a gentle arc, it will begin to drop. Naturally, different bullet weights and calibers have flatter or sharper trajectories and begin their descent at different distances.

Thus, the rifle and carbine shooter's task is to zero their gun and defense ammunition at a reasonable distance. From muzzle contact

Mechanical offset occurs at the close distances likely in home defense, because the sights are located several inches above the barrel, "offsetting" the close range impact. In this illustration, the line from eyes, through the ACOG optical sight and ending on the big black dot, shows the shooter's aiming point, while the actual hit would occur at the point at which the muzzle contacts the target.

distance to the 50-yard zero suggested above, the bullet will rise to intersect with line of sight (the point on the target on which the sights are precisely aligned). Most .223 ammunition will strike only an inch or two higher at the 100-yard line, and begin to drop from that point on.

Training Issues

Besides the pure marksmanship issues associated with carbines, there are additional lessons to be learned if this is the tool with which you intend to defend self and family. One of the biggest impediments to women enjoying rifle shooting is the weight of the gun compared to their upper body strength, not so great an issue for the male shooter. Adaptive techniques that run counter to classic competitive rifle methods can help the female shooter overcome the problem of all that outboard weight.

Perhaps the most simple cure is taking a braced or a kneeling

---- Line of Sight
—— Bullet Trajectory

100 yards

Sighted in for 50 yards

A depiction of bullet trajectory shows the difference between line of sight and actual bullet impact before and beyond the distance at which the rifle is "zeroed." In the drawing, bullet drop is somewhat exaggerated for illustrative purposes.

position whenever possible. Along with stabilizing the gun, it reduces your own target size and should be considered if circumstances allow you to ensconce and fight from a protected position from which you need not move. Along with taking a lower position, be sure the support arm is directly beneath the stock, maximizing skeletal support, as well as exploiting the natural strength of the biceps.

Traditional marksmanship coaches have taught rifle shooters to stand upright, with the rifle centered over legs and feet, shoulders angled back behind hips and the spine in something of an S-curve. This position is very relaxed and perfect for the slow pace of classic competitive courses of fire. Introduce the stress and rapid-fire requirements of a home-defense emergency, however, and the marksman's position deteriorates.

Two decades ago Massad Ayoob developed his combat handgun system, dubbing it StressFire, to indicate techniques that succeed when stress and adrenaline affect the body. He applies many of his basic StressFire principles to the rifle, including taking a tight grip on the rifle and leaning the upper body dramatically forward. A deep, wide stance provides excellent balance and makes the weight of the rifle seem less burdensome. Deeply flex the forward, support-side leg for further stability.

A wide stance helps eliminate the troublesome wobble of the rifle sights across and on and off the target. If sight wobble is unchecked, the shooter usually tries to snatch the trigger when the sights cross the target, a reaction that results in trigger jerk and abysmal accuracy. Instead, Ayoob has developed several radical techniques that further steady the rifle long enough to make an accurate shot.

A strong shooting stance helps shooter stabilize rifle and keep sights on target for accurate hits at greater distances.

Coupled with the StressFire rifle stance, Ayoob teaches a grip modification of which I have made extensive use. Traditionally, the non-dominant hand supports the forend, with the elbow as completely beneath the rifle as possible. This classic shooting technique works for all rifles. When shooting an AR-15, however, I use Ayoob's "Death Grip" method almost exclusively, though it is not recommended for other rifle types on which it may disrupt feeding reliability.

The shooting hand clutches the pistol grip firmly, while the support hand takes a hard grip on the magazine well and pulls firmly. The effect is something like the isometric tension of the Weaver handgun shooting stance, and compensates nicely for limited upper body strength.

An entire book could be written on additional riflery techniques, and indeed many qualified authors have written works worth the reader's time.[1] I present these vignettes in this context to underscore that shooting techniques for most women, whether with a rifle or handgun, must address the particular issues of upper body strength, overall body size and physique, to enhance the female shooter's control on the gun.

The Rifle's Appeal

Evan Marshall believes the rifle fills several roles in civilian self defense. Many people simply find the "long gun" easier to accept. They've been socialized to perceive rifles and shotguns as legitimate, having seen their fathers and grandfathers hunt, he points out. Yet, some are simply unwilling to learn to shoot the shotgun. They've been told the recoil will be painful, and they may be unable to find suitable training. The smaller caliber rifle appeals to this person.

Some jurisdictions still deny citizens the right to own a handgun. Because of the social acceptance of hunting sports, owning a rifle or pistol-caliber carbine may remain permissible. In the wake of strict laws on firearms possession in Canada, we've seen an increase in home invasions and burglaries. As government and society attacks American gun owners' rights, the skills and ability to defend home and family with a less impugned firearm than the handgun may well become vital. Either the shotgun or the rifle, in the hands of a determined, trained individual can do much to assure the safety of innocent citizens and those in their care.

Notes

[1]Suggested reading: *The Fighting Rifle*, Chuck Taylor, 1984; *The Ultimate Sniper, An Advanced Training Manual for Military and Police*, Maj. John L. Plaster, USAR, Ret.1993., both published by Paladin Press, Gunbarrel Tech Center, 7077 Winchester Circle, Colorado 80301. 800-466-6868, 800-392-2400; and *The Farnam Method of Defensive Shotgun and Rifle Shooting*, John S Farnam, DTI Publications, Inc. P. O. Box 18746, Boulder, CO 80308 303-443-9817.

Modifications to classic riflery methods, including what Ayoob teaches as the "Death Grip," ease handling the weight of the carbine.

CHAPTER 24

Post-shooting Survival

I f forced to shoot an assailant in self defense, you should be prepared for a number of consequences, including interacting with the authorities, dealing with your psychological and physiological responses, and answering to a society that may not acknowledge the deadly danger that caused you to use deadly force.

In regard to dealing with the authorities, let's again draw up a hypothetical incident. Home alone, you shoot to stop a knife-wielding criminal who breaks through your bedroom window screaming out his specific, evil intent. The criminal falls and is no longer an immediate threat, so you order him into a controllable posture, face down, hands palms up and fully extended from sides, ankles crossed, his face turned away from you. With the danger of continued attack reduced, you reload your gun and call the police.

He's Down. Now What?

Assume your assailant is still dangerous, even if he has fallen. If he is armed with a contact weapon such as a club or knife, find a position behind furniture that would impede a lunge toward you and keep your gun pointed at the assailant. Maintaining control remains paramount; expect a conscious intruder to resist verbally and physically.

In role play, Kathy faces an assailant brandishing a pipe. She begins with verbal commands, backed up by her Airsoft SIG Sauer. She tells him to drop the weapon, and slowly raise his hands until his elbows are locked and fingers spread.

After the assailant complies, he is ordered to turn slowly and face away. Since he is complying, her finger remains indexed along the side of the SIG's frame.

With the assailant no longer looking at her, Kathy can make an extremely rapid danger scan in case he has accomplices.

Kathy may need to move to keep his hands in sight as he slowly lowers himself to the ground on her command. In this practice scenario, no cover is available, so she could move away at an angle to increase distance.

Assailant is spread-eagled, hands visible, and feet crossed to slow his ability to get up and reinitiate the attack. She will continue to control the assailant until police arrive; the risk remains extreme.

Preparing for the Arrival of the Police

You need to be able to safely put your gun away when police officers arrive. The police have no choice but to consider any gun a threat, because their information is extremely limited. If your assailant is actively threatening, you need to keep your gun pointed at him while preparing to holster or drop the gun if the police order you to do so when they enter the room. Be sure you maintain enough distance to drop the weapon beyond your assailant's reach, and get out of his view so he does not know when you have put the gun away.

Be mentally prepared for the entry of the police officers. This is just one reason to continue talking to the 911 emergency operator until help arrives. If responding officers surprise you and you turn, gun in hand, to see who is coming in, it is likely that you will unintentionally point your gun toward the officers. This may invite gunfire from the police, who cannot automatically determine that you are the innocent party. Don't let a startled response cost your life.

Telling Your Story

You must give the responding officers a truthful account of what occurred. You must not appear secretive or uncooperative, yet must take care to avoid giving confusing information. The catastrophic missteps survivors have made at this point was the impetus to form an organization of which I am one of three founders, the Armed Citizens' Legal Defense Network, LLC.[1] Too often, crime victims who fought back have been charged with assault or murder, and too many of those people were convicted and went to prison for doing what was

The first officer on the scene need only know who attacked you, that you feared for your life, and that the assailant forced your response.

necessary to save their lives. Those who own guns for self defense need a clear understanding of how to report the crime against them that required a deadly force response.

Why not tell the first cops on the scene everything that comes to mind? If you have just survived a look into death's abyss, you will be eager to talk, to make human contact and to justify the horrible act you were forced to commit. The responding officer, who will file an official, court-admissible report, is not the person with whom to share this emotional unburdening. Maintain emotional control. Later, you can bare your soul to a religious advisor or professional counselor to excise the hurt. Details of sessions with priests and psychiatrists are generally exempt from court subpoena, so they're safe resources for post-traumatic event therapy.

There are sound reasons for limiting the information you give to the first law enforcement officer on the scene. Reports of self-defense shootings reveal that the perceptions of trauma survivors are extremely unreliable. A survivor who makes a lengthy statement to the first responder will probably relate incorrect information, especially about exact lengths of time, specific distances and other details. During the stress of a violent encounter, the body and mind narrow their focus to just the threat. This phenomenon, called the tachy psyche effect, causes tunnel vision, distortions in perceptions of time and distance, degradation of fine motor skills, general muscle tightening, and tremors. In addition, hearing shuts down to only that which seems necessary for survival. Called auditory exclusion, this phenomenon causes survivors to report that they did not hear the shots they fired or words yelled by a partner.

The bottom line here is that after an emotionally traumatic event, your memories and perceptions can trick you. Act accordingly! When law enforcement officers arrive at the scene of a self-defense shooting, it is best to supply only general information to avoid reporting inaccurate details as a result of the tachy psyche effect, while emphasizing that a crime was committed against you. If pressed for details at the scene, it is appropriate to tell the questioning officer: "He attacked me. I was forced to shoot before he killed or crippled me. You know how serious this is. I wish to call my attorney before you ask me anything further." By invoking the right to counsel, you cannot be compelled to answer further interrogation. Remember, however, any information freely volunteered, even after requesting legal counsel, can be used against the suspect.

Evan Marshall once told me, "Cops hate to be told 'no,' but it is better for you to spend the night in lockup than 20 years in the penitentiary because of [inaccurate] information you gave right after a shooting."

Even after justifiable police shootings, the involved officer is usually sequestered away from the press and other information seekers, to let him settle his mind and emotions before making a statement or answering questions. You deserve the same consideration, although you may have to insist that you receive it.

Stating the "Active Dynamic"

Have a thoroughly researched survival plan – both against physical attack and to prevent your survival from being seen as a crime. If you ever face this situation, when asked what happened, tell the responding officers, "He broke in and assaulted me. I was forced to shoot to save my life." Ayoob defines this approach as stating "the active dynamic." It truthfully describes what occurred and how the assailant's death or injury occurred.

Compare "He broke in and assaulted me; I was forced to shoot to save my life" to blurting to the first cop on the scene, "He was in the bedroom and I shot him twice." Both statements are true, but the first gives a more accurate picture of who caused the shooting. You had to shoot to stop his assault. A statement underscoring the crime perpetrated against you places responsibility for the outcome squarely on he who initiated the confrontation.

Marshall suggests admitting to fear and a wish to run away. He advises this kind of response to on-the-scene questions: "My first thought was to escape, but that wasn't possible, so I yelled at him to leave. When he came up the stairs toward me and my family, I had to fire in his direction."

At the Police Station

Unless you are hospitalized as a result of the assault, you may be taken into police custody after shooting in self defense. Women are sometimes treated more gently than men, who may find themselves behind bars. You may be allowed only one phone call. Be sure you have laid the groundwork to make that one call productive. You should know, in advance, how to reach your attorney at all hours. This is no time for interference by an answering service paid not to disturb your lawyer during the hours that most self-defense emergencies transpire, i.e., in the dark of night or on weekends.

The best preparation is advance arrangements for a stable family member, trusted associate or friend to contact attorneys and investigators for you. Explain that you want to prepare for the possibility that you might someday need to defend yourself. Ask if they would be willing to help in an emergency, describing for them the events that may follow a self-defense shooting. If they agree to help, it is their number you memorize and you direct your emergency call to them. From their greater freedom and superior privacy, they can call your attorney, a private investigator and anyone else needed to protect your rights during a shooting investigation.

Investigators will likely seize your gun, and probably any other firearms in your home. The police have no way of immediately determining your innocence and may well choose to take custody of any firearms you possess until you are cleared of suspicion. The gun fired will be held as evidence until the prosecutor determines if you will be charged with a crime and through any subsequent court proceedings. It is disturbingly common for victims to have difficulty getting authorities to release firearms thus seized.

And finally, remember that even if authorities decide that there is no reason to charge you with a crime, you may well be sued in civil court by the survivors of the person who assaulted you or by the assailant, if he survives. As incomprehensible as it may seem, rapists' families may surface to argue in court that their "boy" was a good student, active in his church and quite incapable of violence. (By civil court rules of evidence, the plaintiff need only convince the judge or jury that there is a better than 50% chance that their arguments are the truth. In criminal court, evidence must convince the triers of fact "beyond a reasonable doubt," a more demanding burden of truth.)

The judge or jury will be faced with an additional puzzle: you appear before them alive, a survivor. It is sometimes difficult to view the survivor as the real victim. They weigh your vitality against the grief of a bereaved family. An element of sympathy for the dead person or for their survivors is inevitable, in spite of atrocities committed by the deceased.

Attorney Selection

The person who has chosen to possess the power of defensive deadly force needs to have an attorney available, as we just underscored.

Evan Marshall recommends that citizens should understand their legal environment before they must interact with the courts as a defendant. In very small towns, a private law practice may augment the prosecutor's salary. In other instances, find a retired judge or prosecutor who has recently returned to private practice. Marshall suggests making an appointment with this lawyer, and spending an hour asking questions and getting advice about armed self defense and the mood of the court in such cases.

Another alternative Marshall advises is contacting the lawyer who defends the police force after a shooting. This lawyer's connections with the law enforcement community are valuable, he says.

Finally, Marshall concludes, "Know the lay of the land." Local politics, the personal beliefs and the political aspirations of your local prosecutor can influence charges brought against someone who uses force in self defense. Ask the attorney you contact how courts in your area have treated recent self-defense shootings.

Massad Ayoob emphasizes that citizens should not retain a criminal defense attorney, nor should they seek out a famous criminal attorney to lead their defense. He lectures that keeping an attorney on retainer suggests that you expected to shoot someone. Famous criminal attorneys are remembered for "keeping bad guys out of jail," planting the suggestion in jurors' minds that you are not innocent. Instead, he suggests a building a relationship with a retired judge who is likely to be well-connected and understand current judicial attitudes.

Few criminal defense attorneys have experience representing innocent people and may advise you to confess to a crime you did not commit, in exchange for a lenient sentence. A common tactic is pleading that the gun went off accidentally, instead of in an intentional act of self defense. This goes beyond being unwise, beyond being stupid; it is criminal! Not only is a lie given under oath a crime in itself, it compromises the entire self-defense premise, that of the affirmative defense. The self-defense argument asserts that the defendant indeed used deadly force against the assailant. But it also argues that the accused was justified in so doing, as she acted in defense of her own or other innocent life. This is a demanding legal strategy and requires absolute adherence to ethical behavior by both defendant and attorney.

Defense Against an Abusive Partner

You can see that even after a lethal force attack, the survivor faces many ongoing challenges. Preparing for and facing judgment in the courts can be an arduous process, especially in circumstances where the survivor's right to use deadly force is viewed with suspicion by the investigating police or courts. One of the most challenging deadly force scenarios is found in cases where women were forced to kill or injure domestic partners in defense or themselves or their children.

In her book *When Battered Women Kill*[2] author Angela Browne cites a study group of 42 female survivors of domestic abuse and battering, who were charged in the death or serious injury of a husband or boyfriend. Of this group, about half were sentenced to jail terms, twelve received probation or suspended sentences, and only nine were acquitted. Jail sentences ranged from six months to 25 years, and one woman was sentenced to 50 years in prison.

The courts and juries have historically viewed the killing of a domestic partner as an avoidable danger, thus postulating that the homicide must have been "premeditated." Juries lacked the education and sensitivity to recognize that the female survivor's instinct indicated that this time the batterer intended murder, more than the previous battering. Further, the woman's reticence to act against the abusive mate is demonstrated in the time she refrained from taking action against him. If ever expert testimony about abused women's psychology is needed, it is in defense of battered women who kill to save their own or their children's lives.

Your Best Defense Is the Truth

If you are charged with a crime after an act of self defense, your job and the job of your defense team is to show the jury the truth – the information and details that prove you acted in response to an unavoidable threat of death or crippling injury at the hands of an assailant who was committing a crime against you. Entire responsibility for the incident must be shown to rest with the perpetrator. Elements of the defense should include specific information about your training – both marksmanship training and studies in rightful use of lethal force.

Verify that you faced a deadly threat. Demonstrate that you were forced to choose between your life and his. From your first report to the responding officer through testimony in the courtroom, you must always tell the truth. Lies and exaggerations will be uncovered, and if one falsehood is revealed every subsequent statement made becomes dubious. Your justified act of self defense will be tarnished and forever suspect.

Notes

[1] Armed Citizens' Legal Defense Network, LLC., P. O. Box 400, Onalaska, WA 98570 360-978-5200 www.armedcitizensnetwork.org

[2] Browne, Angela, *When Battered Women Kill*, The Free Press, Division of Macmillan, Inc., 1987 pp. 11, 12. Further study: in additional to the above title, home-study resources include *The Ayoob Files*, available from Police Bookshelf, 800-624-9049 and Ayoob's ongoing column The "Ayoob Files" in *American Handgunner* magazine, 619-297-8032. Also contact the Lethal Force Institute, P. O. Box 122, Concord, NH 03302, www.ayoob.com.

Afterword

Two words have received extensive use throughout the foregoing pages: "victim" and "survivor." As this book concludes, take a minute to think about these terms and about yourself. The word "victim" indicates one to whom something is done. The term does not suggest any effective preemptive or defensive action, instead conveying that the person to whom the term is applied is the victim of actions against which she was unwilling or powerless to defend herself.

When "survivor" is used in a sentence, the implication is less black and white. A survivor may have suffered injuries, yet overcome them. Survival occurs on many levels: physical, emotional, spiritual and mental, though the latter are often overlooked in our Western society's preoccupation with the tangible.

Leaders in the field of armed self defense correctly hesitate to employ the term "victor" in describing those who face deadly danger and prevail. It has been suggested that no one "wins" when the worst happens and good people have no alternative but to use lethal force. This view, however, fails to acknowledge the triumphs of preemptive action, of alert avoidance, of verbal intervention and all the other force options we've discussed as ways to avoid criminal attack.

I don't think I could overstate the value of a feminine attitude that, while not seeking out dangers, personifies a woman who is ready, able and willing to use defensive force to prevent injury and abuse to herself and her family. Beyond attitude and belief, this mindset takes form in physical activities such training, personal safety and crime prevention measures, and always remaining alert to unpredictable risks.

This kind of woman is a survivor. Be that survivor.

Keep your head up, keep your spirits up. Stay alert and aware; stay safe.